The Book

Mastering the Algorithm

How to Go Viral, Stay Visible, and Thrive in the Age of Attention

The Book On Series

by Rowan Blake.

Published by The Book On Publishing, 2025.

First edition. July 19, 2025.

Website: https://thebookon.ca

Substack: https://thebookonpublishing.substack.com/

MASTERING THE ALGORITHM: HOW TO GO VIRAL, STAY VISIBLE, AND THRIVE IN THE AGE OF ATTENTION

First edition. July 19, 2025.

Copyright © 2025 The Book On Publishing
ISBN: 978-1-997795-82-7

Written by Rowan Blake.

The Book On Series

Read This First

This is not a book designed to entertain you. It's not here to charm, to soothe, or to hold your hand. It won't dazzle you with stories, metaphors, or motivational fluff. What you're having is a tool, an instruction manual written for people who are serious about learning, executing, and thinking at a higher level.

Every book in The Book On Series is built on a single premise: clarity beats complexity. We believe that when you strip away the noise, the emotions, the marketing spin, and the cultural rituals of "self-help," what's left is raw, unembellished instruction. That's what these books offer.

They are dry by design. Not because we don't care about language or narrative, but because when you're building something that matters, you don't need more distractions. You need a clear architecture. Mental scaffolding. Direction that respects your intelligence.

Each title in this series takes on a specific domain: decision-making, clarity, strategy, leverage, and uncertainty, and drills deep. Not in sweeping generalizations, but in applied frameworks. These are books for builders, operators, founders, tacticians, and thinkers—people who don't just consume knowledge but operationalize it.

You'll find no chapter-long anecdotes here. No self-congratulatory memoirs. No bullet-point platitudes. Instead, what you'll get is structured insight: argument, example, application. The tone is direct. The prose is sober. The ideas are designed to be lifted out and used.

You won't be coddled, but you won't be misled either.

There's a place in the world for lyrical, emotional, story-driven books, and this isn't that place. This is a workspace. A blueprint. A conversation for people who are ready to act, not just absorb.

We respect your time and your intellect.

Welcome to The Book On Series.

Table of Contents

Dedication

For every creator who kept showing up,
even when the algorithm didn't.
This book is for the quiet ones, the thoughtful ones,
and the ones who refuse to trade depth for reach.
Your voice matters.
Keep building.
-R.B.

Acknowledgments

This book began as a question, but it became a conversation, shaped by the generous insights, challenges, and encouragement of many others.

To the creators, writers, designers, and strategists I've had the privilege to learn from: your work helped me see more clearly. To the early readers who offered feedback not just with sharp eyes but with open minds, thank you for helping me make this book what it needed to be.

To the team at The Book On Publishing, your belief in practical, human-centered books made this possible. Thank you for caring more about impact than impressions.

To those closest to me: thank you for grounding me, cheering me on, and reminding me that visibility is never more important than presence.

And to the reader, whether this is your first book on the subject or your fiftieth, thank you for trusting me with your attention. May what you found here support the work only you can make.

Chapter One: Welcome to the Feed

It starts with a scroll. One thumb, one feed, one unconscious ritual. Morning, noon, and night, sometimes all three at once. You're not alone in this. Nearly half the global population taps into social feeds daily, their attention grazing headlines, memes, dopamine triggers, or manufactured controversy. And yet, very few stop to ask: what exactly is this feed? What does it feed on? And perhaps more crucially, who does it feed?

Welcome to the modern Colosseum, where ideas rise and fall in seconds, reputations are made in a day, and silence is a signal. This is not simply a matter of social media strategy. This is a planetary attention system, an evolving architecture of visibility, and you, whether you know it or not, are inside it.

Let's dispense with the platitudes early. This book is not about gaming a platform or hacking the latest algorithm update. It is not about outdoing your neighbor in the engagement game. It's about understanding the system beneath the system, the infrastructure of attention itself, and deciding how you intend to navigate it, shape it, or be consumed by it.

Because the algorithm, despite its omnipresence in cultural discourse, is not one single thing. It is not a monolithic entity, even if we talk about it that way. The algorithm is an evolving series of predictive models, behavioral feedback loops, and human-engineered proxies for value. It is trained not just on your clicks and likes, but also on your hesitations, the time you spend on each item, silent scrolling, and re-watching. It learns from what you do, not what you say. It reacts faster than you can formulate an intention.

But what makes this moment unique, what makes now different from five years ago, is not just that algorithms shape our feeds. It's what feeds and shapes our realities. Our perception of success, popularity, credibility, and even truth is increasingly dictated by what surfaces on a screen. If you are not visible, you are not trusted. If you are not repeated, you are not believed. And if you are not viral, you are presumed irrelevant.

That's a brutal calculus. And yet, it's the game. So the real question isn't whether you should play. The question is: how do you play in a way that doesn't annihilate your integrity, your time, or your sanity? And even deeper than that, how do you stay seen without becoming hollow?

The truth is, most people don't. Most creators burn out before they break out. Most entrepreneurs mistake reaching for resonance. And most professionals still cling to the myth that doing good work is enough to be discovered. It isn't. It never has been. Not in a noisy world. Not in an infinite feed.

So, let's start from here: the feed is not neutral. It is not merely showing you what is "popular." It is constructing a dynamic map of attention, based on invisible calculations you'll never see. And the more you understand how it works, how it's built, how it responds, how it adapts, the more you can reclaim your agency within it.

This isn't a conspiracy theory. It's a systems theory. Every platform's feed is an evolving experiment in behavioral engineering. YouTube optimizes for retention and watch time, training you to stay in session longer. Instagram responds to early engagement velocity, rewarding posts that spike quickly with exponential reach. TikTok favors novelty and completion rate, often ignoring follower count altogether. LinkedIn pushes content that sparks professional responses, comments, reposts, and debates. These aren't design quirks. They're strategic imperatives baked into trillion-dollar ecosystems.

In short, you are not posting content into a void. You are throwing your ideas into a predictive machine, and that machine is not just analyzing your content; it is analyzing you. What time do you post? How often. Whether you interact. How fast your audience responds. Whether your voice is consistent or chaotic. Whether people swipe away or linger. The machine is listening. Always.

And here's the real kicker: it's not listening to reward you. It's listening to optimize itself.

The machine does not care about fairness, originality, or even truth. It cares about patterns. Attention patterns. Retention patterns. It is fed by behavior, and it feeds you back what it thinks you will act on. The rest is discarded. Not penalized, just rendered invisible. Which is, in the economy of attention, the same thing as being erased.

So, if you feel like your voice is being drowned out, you're not paranoid. You're right. The digital landscape is designed to amplify predictability and marginalize nuance. And that has profound consequences, not just for content creators or marketers, but for anyone trying to make an idea matter.

If you're still reading, then you already know this. You feel it. You've probably seen good work ignored while mediocre posts explode. You've watched unoriginal trends go viral while complex insights gather dust. You've posted something meaningful, only to see it vanish into algorithmic oblivion while someone else gains traction by mimicking memes.

This book is about what to do next.

It's about navigating a world where algorithms not only distribute content but also determine perception. Where being strategic isn't cynical, it's necessary. Where depth and reach don't have to be enemies, but where they often are. It's about reclaiming visibility without losing your voice.

And it starts right here, in the feed, in the flicker, in the chaos. Welcome.

The first step in reclaiming visibility is to stop waiting for the algorithm to "favor" you. That sort of thinking, hopeful, passive, externalized, is a form of surrender. It's no different than waiting for a literary agent to pluck your manuscript out of a slush pile or for a record label to discover your garage band. We've seen this before. The gatekeepers are gone, but the psychological habits remain. Too many talented people still think they need permission to be seen.

They don't. Not anymore.

In this new landscape, visibility is not granted. It is constructed. Intentionally. Deliberately. Pattern by pattern.

That doesn't mean everyone can become viral. The internet is not a meritocracy, nor is virality a reliable reward for quality. But everyone can become visible to the right people if they approach their presence with clarity and repetition.

Let's take a detour here, because this matters: visibility is not the same as fame. The obsession with virality often masks a more profound truth: that most successful people online are not famous; they are just consistently visible within the circles that matter. A B2B consultant with 12,000 LinkedIn followers might drive more impact, revenue, and opportunity than a Twitter account with 400,000 followers and no focus. A designer posting twice weekly to 3,000 engaged Instagram followers might quietly run a million-dollar design agency. They are not trying to go viral. They are trying to be unmistakable.

This book isn't about chasing scale. It's about building gravity.

The feed rewards gravity. That's a truth nobody tells you. While the platforms change, and the metrics shift, what doesn't change is this: the more clearly you project who you are, what you do, and why it matters, the more likely the machine is to recognize you as a "signal" rather than noise.

And here's the twist: the algorithm doesn't create virality. You do. You make it by showing up in a way that teaches the system what kind of object you are. The more consistent your signal, the faster the system learns where to route your work.

Let's use a metaphor.

Imagine a massive neural map of the internet. Millions of signals are fired every second: photos, videos, captions, shares. The algorithm is a routing system, a probabilistic guessing engine. It attempts to determine which users are most likely to engage with specific signals. If your signal is clear, the system routes it more confidently. If your signal is erratic, it hesitates. It slows. It throttles. It waits for confirmation.

This is why inconsistency kills. Not just posting inconsistency, but inconsistency of message, of tone, of identity. One day, you're posting memes. The following are deep thoughts on economic inequality. The next is a promo for your coaching business. And you wonder why your reach is unpredictable.

It's not about the content type. It's about how you train the machine to interpret what you're sending. Content doesn't just exist in isolation. It lives in a probabilistic matrix of expectations. You're not posting in a diary. You're communicating in a lattice of signals, history, and modeled behavior. The machine decides what you are based on your patterns, not your intentions.

That's not unfair. It's just mechanical.

And it's the reason why people who "do one thing well" seem to rise faster online than those who try to be dynamic. In real life, we love complexity. Online, complexity looks like incoherence. The feed is a reductionist medium. It rewards the clearest signal, not the richest one. That's why the most successful creators often look simple at first glance but are anything but. Their simplicity is engineered. It's the result of knowing which thread to pull and pulling it endlessly until it becomes unmistakable.

So let me offer this reframing: your goal is not to get the algorithm to notice you. Your goal is to teach the algorithm who you are, with such clarity, frequency, and predictability that it begins to associate your presence with a specific pattern of value.

You don't want to be a surprise. You want to be a shortcut.

This is why early traction often looks like luck but isn't. It's the outcome of invisible training, weeks or months of consistent signaling that culminate in a tipping point. When that moment hits, the system doesn't just notice you. It finally understands you. And once it does, it begins to favor you, not because of magic, but because of math. You've made yourself legible to the machine.

14

And here's the more profound truth: you've made yourself legible to the audience, too.

Human attention follows similar rules. People trust what they see often. They engage with what they understand. And they remember what they can describe easily. "She's the guy who always posts those clean visual explainers." "He's the one who writes those savage takes on startup culture." "She's the strategist who breaks down platform shifts better than anyone." That kind of association doesn't happen by accident. It happens through engineered repetition.

This doesn't mean becoming robotic. It means becoming intentional. It means understanding that online, clarity is identity.

Too many people resist this. They want to be complex. They want to be taken seriously. They think repetition will flatten their nuance. But the opposite is true. Repetition is what allows nuance to emerge. It gives you the freedom to deepen over time, because the audience already knows what to expect. It gives you the right to evolve, because they know your baseline.

Without that, you're just another unknown signal in a sea of noise.

So, if you want to be seen, don't wait for virality. Don't plead with the algorithm. Train it. Teach it. Make yourself a recognizable object within the machine.

Because once the system knows what you are, it begins to carry you further. Not out of kindness. Not out of justice. But because it finally knows where you belong.

And that's when visibility stops being a chase and becomes gravity.

Before we move on...

There is one more truth to confront before we leave this chapter, and it's the most uncomfortable one: visibility in this system is not only constructed, it is also comparative. You are not just trying to be seen; you are trying to be seen instead of something else. Every impression you gain is one someone else doesn't. Every second you hold attention is time stolen from another signal. In a finite attention economy, growth always carries displacement.

This may feel adversarial. Unfair. Cutthroat. But it's simply the nature of competitive systems. If the algorithm is a sorting engine, then it must sort. And sorting requires choice. So your presence online is not evaluated in isolation; it is evaluated in context. It is weighed against what else could be shown in your place.

This is why "quality" is not enough. Plenty of people post quality content. The feed is littered with brilliance that went nowhere. The question is not just: is this good? It's: Is this better than the next best thing the algorithm could serve? Is it more clickable than the meme? More interesting than the trending video? More relevant than the user's notifications?

You're not just competing with others in your niche. You're competing with everything else the machine could show: sports clips, Master news, influencer drama, and cat videos. You are in the fight of your life for a few milliseconds of thumb-stopping power.

And yet, this isn't a call to sell out. It's not a suggestion to become louder, dumber, or more provocative. The lowest common denominator trap is real, and anyone can go viral once for the wrong reasons. But that's not the kind of visibility you

16

want. That's noise masquerading as reach. It's unsustainable. It burns fast and leaves nothing behind.

What you want is strategic visibility. Repeatable visibility. The kind that compounds over time, rather than exploding and evaporating. And that only comes from building a system, not just a style.

Your system starts with signal clarity, but it's also about behavioral coherence. Do you post regularly? Do you engage with your audience? Do you create a rhythm that the algorithm can detect? Do you present an identity that people can easily summarize, share, and associate with?

And deeper still, do you create work that feels like it belongs on the platform, while still feeling unmistakably yours?

This is the nuance most people miss. The algorithm doesn't reward originality in the abstract. It rewards familiarity within context. In other words, your work must look native to the platform while being unique within it. A tweet that sounds like a tweet, but only you could have written. A reel that looks like a reel but carries your voice unmistakably. This is the tightrope you walk. Too much sameness, and you become invisible. Too much deviation, and you confuse the system.

That's why strategic creators don't just think about content. They think about containers. They ask: What is the shape of content that wins here? What is the format the system understands? And then: how do I fill that container with something nobody else can?

This is the real art. It's not gaming the algorithm. It's understanding its preferences well enough to deliver something of value, consistently, authentically, and within the rules of the medium.

And once you understand that, you begin to shift from participant to architect. You stop reacting to algorithm changes and start building with them. You stop chasing trends and start setting your cadence. You stop complaining about the lack of reach and start asking better questions about what the system is optimizing for and how you can align with it without losing your soul.

Because that's the final risk in this game, if you're not careful, the pursuit of visibility can become an act of erasure. You can slowly shape-shift into something palatable, safe, algorithmically compatible, but no longer real. And that is a kind of death. Not digital death. Creative death.

And make no mistake: the platforms will let you trade authenticity for reach. They will reward predictability over innovation. They will push you toward content patterns that are easier to digest and easier to monetize. They don't care if you become a caricature of yourself, as long as you produce a signal on schedule. They will let you feed the machine until it hollows you out.

Don't let it.

This book is not about conformity. It's about clarity. It's about designing a presence that is both system-aware and self-directed. It's about building a visible identity without becoming invisible to yourself.

Because in the end, Mastering The Algorithm doesn't mean tricking the system. It means becoming so coherent, so legible, so consistently valuable that the system has no choice but to surface you. Not once. Not randomly. But repeatedly.

It means building presence with precision, not waiting for luck, and not reacting to chaos, but creating conditions where gravity starts to work in your favor, where your presence becomes a pattern the machine wants to repeat.

So welcome to the feed. You are now aware of the game. And whether you choose to engage with it actively or passively, you are already in it. Every post. Every scroll. Every silence. Every signal.

The next step is simple, but not easy.

You must decide what you want to be known for, and then become so clear, so consistent, so aligned with that signal that both humans and machines can't ignore it.

That is how you break the algorithm.

And that is where we begin.

Chapter Two: The Psychology of Attention

If you want to win in the economy of attention, you must first understand what attention is. Not just as a buzzword or a marketing metric, but as a biological function, a psychological limitation, and a social currency. Attention is not something people give freely. It is something they lose, over and over again, until something sharp enough or relevant enough takes hold.

This is why we say things like "grab attention" or "capture interest." It's not a coincidence. Attention is a finite resource that must be claimed. In the digital world, it's not just finite, it's fractured, frenzied, and always in flux.

But attention isn't merely a matter of time spent. That's a common mistake. Platforms might measure it in seconds, but what they're chasing is **cognitive arousal**, a spike in the brain's awareness that signals "this matters." That spike can come from novelty, beauty, outrage, intimacy, threat, or clarity. It doesn't matter what causes it. What matters is that something cut through the fog.

And that fog is thicker than ever.

In an environment of infinite content, attention becomes an act of triage. Your audience is not evaluating your content in isolation; they're considering whether it is more urgent than the other dozen inputs flying at them that very second. Push notifications, trending alerts, DMs, banners, overlays, autoplay videos. In this chaos, the brain doesn't make rational decisions. It makes snap judgments based on pattern recognition, emotional triggers, and a hardwired preference for survival.

To navigate this, you need more than a content strategy. You need an **attention strategy**.

That means understanding what your audience is paying attention to, and more importantly, why.

Let's pull this apart.

Humans pay attention to things that signal **change**. We are pattern-seeking creatures, but we're wired to detect disruption. A loud noise in the forest. A strange face in the crowd. A sudden movement in a quiet room. The brain tunes out the expected and focuses sharply on the unexpected.

This is why predictability alone is not enough to win attention. You can't just post on a schedule and expect people to care. You need contrast. You need punctuation. You need something that jolts the system just enough to be noticed, but not so much that it confuses the brain and gets discarded.

This is the paradox: people want familiarity, but they pay attention to novelty. You need to give them both.

And here's where most people fail. They mistake novelty for randomness. They throw spaghetti at the wall. They confuse "keeping it fresh" with having no discernible identity. But true novelty only works *inside a recognizable frame*. The reason a plot twist lands in a film is that you first established a coherent storyline. The twist means nothing without the pattern. Surprise only works when there is something to disrupt.

So, in the context of content and visibility, your job is to build a frame, then break it at just the right moments.

This is why the best creators don't just post content. They build anticipation. Their audience knows what kind of value to expect, and then every so often, they drop something unexpected, a personal story, a raw confession, a sharp take that breaks the rhythm. And that break lands with force because it's set up by weeks or months of pattern.

But let's go deeper.

Attention is also a function of **emotional resonance**. People don't remember data. They remember how something made them feel. Aesthetic beauty, moral anger, shared identity, cleverness, vulnerability: these are emotional levers, and they are everywhere in the most effective online content.

And yet, too many creators build like engineers. They optimize for structure, logic, and clarity, but often overlook the importance of emotional friction. The result is content that's technically sound, but cognitively dull. It might be correct. It might even be helpful. But it never lodges itself in the brain.

What you need is texture. You need content that lives in the emotional layer, not just the informational one.

Think about the content that has stayed with you. A phrase you couldn't forget. A story that hits you in the chest. A tweet that felt like it was written directly to your past self. That's not content. That's contact. That's the emotional hook that makes people not just consume but *remember*.

That's what you're aiming for.

And to get there, you must also confront the role of **identity** in attention. People don't just pay attention to what is interesting. They pay attention to what affirms their identity or challenges it. In other words, if your content makes them feel more like who they already believe they are, or dares them to re-evaluate, it creates tension. And tension is attention.

This is why tribal content works, why ideology spreads faster than nuance. Why the simplest memes sometimes outperform the deepest essays. Because they make people feel like they *belong*, or they *don't*, and both states create energy.

As a strategic communicator, you must choose how you interact with identity. Do you affirm your audience's self-concept? Do you challenge it? Do you reflect it on them in sharper resolution?

But whatever you do, you must not ignore it. Content that floats in a vacuum, free of emotional and identity resonance, dies. No one is thinking about your message in a lab. They are thinking about it in a sea of feelings, memories, self-perceptions, and tribal affiliations. You either tap into that, or you get tuned out.

This is the work.

It's not about shouting louder. It's about speaking in ways that register, neurologically, emotionally, and socially. It's about becoming legible to both the brain and the heart. Because that's where attention lives, and that's where ideas go to either die or grow.

And now that you understand this, you're ready to begin crafting not just content, but signal.

Signal that the algorithm recognizes. A signal that the audience remembers. A signal that is not just another noise in the feed, but a thread they want to pull.

Because the truth is, attention is never truly "captured." It's earned. Over time. Through texture, tension, and repetition.

The good news?

That's something you can learn to do.

To truly master attention, you need to shift from asking "What should I post?" to asking "What does this cause someone to feel, remember, or do?" This subtle reorientation changes everything. It moves you out of the content creator mindset and into the attention architect mindset. And architecture, unlike decoration, is about function. It's about what a thing does, not just what it looks like.

Let's revisit the nature of attention from this new perspective. Attention is not a passive state. It's not someone sitting back and observing your work like they're in a gallery. It's an active exchange of cognitive energy. When someone gives you attention, even momentarily, they are sacrificing something else, another piece of content, another thought, another scroll. Your job isn't just to fill that space. Your job is to reward the sacrifice.

This is where so many well-meaning creators go wrong. They assume that putting something out, anything, is progress. That visibility itself is a victory. But this is false. Visibility without resonance is noise. It may be measurable, but it's not meaningful. What matters is what the attention leads to.

Did it lead to understanding? Did it lead to action? Did it lead to a shift in perception? If not, what you had wasn't attention; it was an interruption.

We've all seen this in the wild. A video with 200,000 views and no engagement. A viral tweet that yields nothing for the person who wrote it. A post with high impressions but zero replies, no clicks, and no memory the next day. That's not visibility. That's disposable exposure.

If you want to build something real, you must optimize not just for reach, but for retention, not just for awareness, but for attachment. You want to create what psychologists call salience, that sticky, lingering mental presence that makes someone think about your work hours after they've left the screen.

How do you create salience?

By designing your content as a trigger, not just a statement. Something that prompts the user to reconsider their knowledge, reframe their current situation, or feel suddenly understood. You're not trying to fill a feed. You're trying to insert a mental wedge that opens the door for more attention later. Salience is what turns passive viewers into followers, and followers into participants.

But salience requires sharpness. You don't get there by being vague. You don't get there by copying trends. You get there by saying something clean enough to remember and true enough to feel, which means stripping away jargon, softening qualifiers, and committing to a point of view.

Point of view is not opinion. It's the worldview behind your work. It's the lens through which your audience sees your content and understands what you stand for. Without a point of view, your content is just noise. A repetition of data points, quotes, and empty encouragement. It might look good. It might even go viral from time to time. But it won't build gravity. It won't anchor you in anyone's mental map.

And anchoring is what matters now.

In an era where every platform is flooded, your presence only becomes meaningful when people can locate you in their inner attention graph. "She's the one who breaks things down like no one else." "He's the guy who always says what others won't."

"They're the ones who blend psychology with tech without ever sounding robotic."

These are not surface impressions. They are tags. Cognitive shortcuts that the brain uses to filter future inputs. And they don't form by accident. They form because you've shown up consistently with a signal that reinforces the same associations, over and over again.

That's why you must resist the temptation to be endlessly flexible. Yes, you can discuss more than one topic. But every new direction adds cognitive friction. Every new angle dilutes the sharpness of the last. If your content feels like a buffet, people will browse. If it feels like a signature dish, they'll come back.

Now, let's touch on the role of **contrast**. One of the most overlooked tools in attention design is the power of comparison, not just visual, but conceptual. Contrast is what creates clarity. If everything in the feed is polished, a raw post stands out. If everything is chaotic, simplicity shines. If everyone is mimicking each other, originality becomes radical.

This is why sameness is a trap. The more your content blends into the current trend, be it design, tone, or format, the more invisible it becomes. Platforms reward familiarity, yes, but only when it's layered over differentiation. This is the creative tension you must hold. Familiar format. Unexpected content. Familiar tone. Unusual insight.

Remember: the brain tunes out what it's already seen. So your job is to work within the language of the platform but speak in a dialect all your own.

A single sentence can do this.

Think of a post that stops you cold. Not because it was flashy, but because it said something you hadn't put into words yet. That's not an accident. That's authorship. That's design. The person who wrote it wasn't just trying to be seen; they were trying to give you a thought you could carry.

That's the goal. Not just reach, not just engagement, but mental imprint. Something portable. Something sticky.

This is why tone matters. You don't need to be loud to be memorable. You need to be precise. You need to speak in a voice that people can hear without effort and recognize instantly. A great voice doesn't shout. It whispers something only your ideal audience is ready to listen to.

And once they hear it, they're marked.

That's what real attention feels like. Not a spike in views. Not a bump in likes. But a private moment of alignment. A reader or viewer saying: This is it. This is the person who gets it.

If you do this once, you earn a follow. If you do this often, you build a brand. And if you do it relentlessly, you stop being a voice in the crowd and start becoming a reference point.

A node. A symbol. A name people cite when they talk about clarity.

That is the true power of earned attention.

And that's what we'll build, one clear, resonant signal at a time.

There's something rarely spoken about in conversations around digital visibility, something more profound than content formats, timing tricks, or platform mechanics. It's not flashy. It's not easily commodified. But it's the quiet thread running through every person who commands attention in a meaningful way.

That something is coherence, internal, mental, and emotional coherence.

It begins long before the first post goes live or the camera turns on. Long before the voice is sharpened, or the audience starts to grow. It begins in the invisible choices a person makes each day, what they allow in, what they protect, and what they're willing to pursue when no one's looking. Because no matter how cleverly crafted the output, it always carries the signature of the mind that shaped it.

And in this age of acceleration, that signature either signals depth or it doesn't. It either carries weight or it floats like everything else.

The truth is, most people trying to earn attention online are drowning in the very system they're trying to stand out in. They consume endlessly, scroll reactively, mimic thoughtlessly, then wonder why their voice feels thin. It's because attention, before it's something you earn from others, is something you must first master in yourself.

The brain wasn't built for twenty open tabs, endless notifications, and algorithmically curated overwhelm. And yet we've accepted this as usual. We train ourselves to respond, not to reflect. We flick from app to app with the glazed eyes of someone lost in a hall of mirrors, not realizing that every one of those mirrors distorts. Over time, this fragmentation doesn't just exhaust you, it changes you. It makes you reactive. Impatient. Imprecise.

And this imprecision bleeds into everything you create.

The clearest thinkers, the ones whose words seem to cut through fog, aren't necessarily more talented. They're simply less scattered. They've cultivated quiet. Not always by retreating, but by refusing to let the chaos dictate their pace. You can feel it in their work. There's air in it. There's weight.

They don't try to say everything. They say the thing that matters.

This clarity is not found by accident. It is practiced. A habit of returning, again and again, to the core of what one knows, believes, or is trying to find out, and not chasing novelty. Not shape-shifting with every trend, but drilling patiently into the essence.

That's what gives a message gravity. Not loudness. Not reach. Not even Polish. But depth earned through attention that's been wrestled with, shaped, and honed. When someone with that kind of presence speaks, you lean in. Not because they command you to, but because you sense that they are not lost. And in a world addicted to noise, coherence is magnetic.

You can't fake this. Not for long.

You might go viral. You might build a following. But without depth, it crumbles. The audience may still be there, but the signal they once felt starts to fade. You see it in creators who explode too fast and implode even quicker. The system gave them attention before they were ready to hold it. And when they reached for more, there was nothing underneath.

That emptiness doesn't come from lack of effort. It comes from the absence of a foundation.

And the foundation is always built in silence. In the days no one sees. In the books you return to, the questions you won't let go of, the ideas you can't shake. It's what anchors you when the metrics dip. It's what keeps your voice intact when the algorithm shifts. It's what makes you still worth listening to, even when the crowd moves on.

This, perhaps, is the most incredible illusion of the digital age: that speed equals relevance. That volume equals value. That more is better.

But the ones who last, the ones whose words keep getting quoted, whose ideas show up in other people's mouths, whose presence carries weight long after the post is forgotten, are not the ones who move the fastest.

They're the ones who stay grounded when everything else spins.

And this is why the real work of building attention-worthy presence is not external. It's internal. It's not about how much you know, but how deeply you've thought. It's not about being interesting; it's about being anchored. People don't just want content. They want contact with someone who seems to know who they are.

If you can be that, if you can cultivate the kind of clarity that's rooted in something more profound than trends, then the system, over time, begins to work for you. Not because you tricked it. But because you taught it that your signal is worth repeating.

And when the platform recognizes that, when the audience feels that, they return.

Not just because they want to consume you.

But because they trust you not to waste their time.

That is what attention, in its most valid form, really means.

Chapter Three: Building Signal

By now, it should be clear that attention isn't random. It doesn't favor the loudest, the newest, or even the most talented. It favors the most recognizable signals, the ones that repeat, reinforce, and settle into the brain like a familiar rhythm. This is the next stage in your evolution from participant to presence: building signal, not simply creating content.

The distinction is crucial. Content is what fills the feed. Signal is what teaches the system what you are. And in a landscape as saturated and competitive as the one we now inhabit; the algorithm doesn't need more content. It needs clarity. The feed is not looking for brilliance in isolation; it's scanning for patterns it can classify, prioritize, and distribute. What you post matters, yes, but what matters more is what the machine learns from your behavior over time. The question is no longer "Did this perform?" It is "What does this tell the system about who I am, and should I be shown again?"

To build a signal, you have to become legible. Legibility is not simplicity. It is not dumbing yourself down or sanding off your edges. It is the ability to be recognized, categorized, and routed, not only by the algorithm, but by the human minds that co-exist with it. You become legible when someone can glance at your work, your profile, or your presence and know what you stand for, what you're trying to say, and what kind of value you offer. This clarity isn't just stylistic. It's strategic. It becomes the foundation of your visibility.

This is why the best creators are often mistaken for being repetitive. They are not repeating themselves out of laziness or lack of ideas. They are repeating themselves with precision because they understand what signal-building requires. It requires patterns. It requires hooks. It requires discipline to stay on message even when the temptation to diversify is strong. The creator who can articulate the same idea in fifty ways is not stagnant. They are memorable.

You've likely heard the saying that people need to listen to a message multiple times before they absorb it. The marketing world tends to frame this as the "Rule of Seven." But in the age of fractured attention, seven is generous. With the speed and chaos of today's feeds, you may need to show up with the same signal dozens of times before the system and the audience truly understand what you are. This isn't redundancy. It's signal reinforcement. It's training the machine and the human mind behind the screen to recognize your shape.

Shape is the right word here, because signal is not just what you say. It's the whole silhouette of your presence, your tone, your rhythm, your visuals, your structure, your timing. It's the entire constellation of choices that, over time, form an identity in the digital environment. That identity doesn't need to be loud. It doesn't need to be provocative. But it does need to be consistent. And more importantly, it needs to be designed.

Design, in this context, is not aesthetics. It's intentionality. It's the difference between posting what you feel like today versus showing up in a way that strengthens your pattern. It's not inauthentic. It's the most honest thing you can do, because it treats your presence as a craft, not a compulsion. You're not just speaking. You're building. And what you build becomes recognizable only when you stop reacting and start composing.

Composing a signal doesn't require being perfect. It requires being clear. Clarity does not mean that every post lands. It doesn't mean every video performs. It means that everything you put into the world stacks in the same direction. One misfire won't cost you much. But fifty scattershot pieces with no through-line won't just slow you down; they'll teach the system that you're incoherent. And once that impression is formed, it isn't easy to undo.

This is why consistency matters more than frequency. You don't need to post every day. But when you do post, it needs to point toward the same shape. You need to reinforce the signal you've chosen, not because the algorithm demands it, but because the audience forgets. No one is thinking about your brand when they wake up. No one is keeping track of your themes. If you don't remind them, they won't remember. If you don't anchor your signal, it will drift. And if it drifts too far, it might not be recognized at all.

Of course, there's a fear that repetition will bore your audience. Saying the same thing in new ways can make you predictable. But this fear misunderstands the game. You are not creating for people who have consumed your entire archive. You are creating for people who are encountering you for the first time today. And tomorrow. And next week. The feed is always onboarding. New eyes arrive with every post, every share, every recommendation. Repetition isn't for your longtime followers. It's for the strangers just beginning to see you.

And even for those who have followed you for a while, repetition is not a flaw. It's a feature. In a world of fleeting impressions, reinforcement is a gift. It gives people something to hold onto, to describe, to reference. It's how you move from content creator to category owner, someone who doesn't just participate in conversations but defines their shape.

You don't get there by accident. You get there by shaping a signal deliberately, over time, until it becomes impossible to mistake you for anyone else.

There is a moment, in the progression of every meaningful voice, when a quiet shift occurs. It's not marked by a viral post or a sudden follower spike. It happens invisibly, often without fanfare, and yet it changes everything. The shift is from being consumed sporadically to being anticipated. The moment when people don't just notice what you've said today, but begin to look forward to what you'll say next. That is the point at which you cease to be a node in the feed and start becoming a fixed point in someone's intellectual landscape.

This shift doesn't happen because you've mastered content. It happens because you've built a signal that persists. That signal is not just informational, it's relational. People begin to associate you with a specific kind of insight, mood, or energy. Your name becomes shorthand for a particular feeling, a trusted lens through which they can view a chaotic world. The audience is no longer checking in on your work. They're using your work to check in on themselves.

This is what the best creators, thinkers, and strategists achieve, not through tricks or frequency hacks, but through the slow accrual of clarity over time. They stay in orbit long enough and consistently enough that the gravity of their presence begins to pull. And once gravity forms, everything changes. The effort shifts from chasing attention to sustaining it. From initiating visibility to managing it. And from being one of many to being the one people remember.

But to reach that place, you must resist the urge to reinvent yourself every few weeks. Reinvention might feel like creative expression, but it's often a symptom of impatience or insecurity. The impulse to change directions too frequently is usually born from doubt, doubt that the current signal is enough, doubt that repetition is valuable, or doubt that the audience will wait. But doubt distorts your ability to build something lasting. It tempts you to throw away what you've built for the illusion of momentum.

There is a kind of power in staying put. Not in a literal sense, evolution is essential, but in the more profound, strategic understanding of remaining legible to your audience while you grow. You can evolve your content. You can refine your tone. But the underlying shape of your signal must remain traceable. If your audience can't describe you in a sentence, they can't share you. And if they can't share you, your growth depends entirely on your effort. That's not a system. That's a treadmill.

Systems are what let you grow without burning out. A system is more than a schedule. It's a set of reinforcing patterns that teach both the algorithm and your audience how to classify you. When you show up with consistency in tone, structure, and subject matter, your posts begin to surface more easily. The feed recognizes the pattern and leans toward it. Your audience learns what to expect and how to interact. This is the architecture of visibility, and it's built not through volume, but through intelligent repetition.

Think about how people recommend others. It's rarely through a comprehensive description. It's almost always a sentence. "She's the one who explains complex tech without the jargon." "He's the guy who breaks down marketing in a way that makes sense." "They're the account that always gives you something to think about." These aren't accidental summaries. They are the byproduct of a reinforced signal.

The question you must ask yourself regularly is this: What would people say about me in that sentence?

If the answer is vague, your signal needs sharpening. If the answer changes week to week, your audience doesn't have a reliable tag to attach to your work. And if you don't provide the tag, the algorithm won't either.

At this stage, building a signal becomes a creative challenge. Not how to be louder, but how to be more *you*. How to double down on your style, your phrasing, your insight, until what you create becomes unmistakable. This doesn't require gimmicks. It doesn't need branding overlays, rigid color palettes, or forced slogans. What it requires is trust. Trust in your ability to delve deeper into the themes that matter to you, exploring them from various angles without losing the core of your message.

The creators who develop gravity are the ones who follow their curiosity within a frame. They don't abandon their signal to chase every passing trend. They respond to the moment, yes, but always through their lens. This lens is what gives them coherence. It's what allows them to touch on many subjects while still feeling like themselves. Their signal isn't a topic; it's a perspective. And a well-honed perspective can follow you across platforms, formats, and even industries.

This is why personal brands that endure often feel like categories of one. They may speak about productivity, or culture, or design, but what draws people in is not the topic. It's the texture. The way their mind works. The emotional resonance that comes through in their voice is palpable. The cadence, the timing, the word choice. All of it adds up to something recognizable.

Recognition is the beginning of trust. And trust is the beginning of influence.

The platforms won't tell you this. They'll point to metrics, views, likes, and reach as if those are the indicators that matter most. But those numbers are temporary. They tell you who saw you. They don't tell you who remembered you. And they certainly don't tell you who would miss you if you stopped posting tomorrow.

Signal is what fills that gap. It turns visibility into memory. It turns exposure into presence.

And once presence is formed, you stop playing the same game as everyone else.

You stop trying to be found.

You become the one people come looking for.

What happens after the signal becomes strong enough to attract attention on its own? For many, this is where momentum begins to shift. But paradoxically, it's also where most falter. Because sustaining a signal is not a matter of simply repeating what worked, it's about reinforcing the trust you've built without becoming stale. It's about cultivating evolution without sacrificing identity.

The most successful presences online are not static. They are dynamic but coherent. They evolve in public, but they do so within a framework that remains recognizable. There's a certain restraint involved, not in expression, but in strategy. The restraint lies in not trying to be everything to everyone, even as doors begin to open and attention starts to scale.

There will come a moment when you're tempted to pivot sharply. To expand beyond your lane, to leverage your attention into new areas. Sometimes that temptation is rooted in growth, in boredom, or sometimes in fear. And while there is nothing inherently wrong with expansion, you must learn to differentiate between strategic evolution and opportunistic drift.

Drift happens when you abandon your signal to chase something shiny. Evolution occurs when your signal deepens into something broader but still anchored. The key to navigating this is to revisit the core reasons why your signal took hold in the first place. What emotional space did you occupy in your audience's mind? What utility did you deliver that others didn't? What tone, what texture, what rhythm became associated with your work?

These are not cosmetic details. They are the connective tissue of your presence. And if you lose them, you may gain short-term novelty but lose long-term coherence. The audience might still watch. The algorithm might still surface you. But something will feel off. You'll sense it in the comments, in the engagement, in the slow erosion of resonance.

This is where self-awareness becomes more than a virtue. It becomes a requirement. Because building a signal is not a one-time effort, it's a constant process of alignment. A cycle of listening to how your work lands, reflecting on whether it reflects your actual intent, and adjusting just enough to stay sharp without becoming erratic.

And yes, this is work. But it's the kind of work that compounds. With every post, every article, every video or podcast episode that reinforces your signal, you deepen the grooves in the audience's mental map. You become more than a creator. You become a reference point. People start to cite you, to quote you, to mimic your phrasing. Not because you gamed the system, but because you embodied something worth returning to.

And from that place, the way you interact with the algorithm begins to shift. You stop needing to chase virality because your presence begins to carry its momentum. This doesn't mean you'll never have a quiet day. It doesn't mean every post will land. But the cumulative weight of your signal ensures that visibility is no longer accidental. It's patterned. Trained. Embedded.

You might start to see that your best-performing work isn't always the flashiest. It's the most resonant. It's the post that distilled something everyone felt but hadn't yet articulated. The one that hit with such clarity that it started showing up in screenshots, in conversations, in strategy decks. That kind of content doesn't rely on format. It depends on the truth. And truth, when paired with repetition and clarity, becomes unignorable.

Unignorable presence is the opposite of attention-hacking. It's not a trick. It's not a campaign. It's a presence that people trust to deliver a particular kind of value, and who do so with enough consistency that their feed begins to feel incomplete without it. That's what makes the difference between the accounts you follow and forget, and the ones you follow and cite.

This kind of presence can be built. But it requires discipline.

Discipline to resist noise. Discipline to stay on theme when it's tempting to swerve. Discipline to refine your thinking, even when others are filling the feed with fluff. Discipline to remain consistent in tone and presence even when the performance metrics wobble. Discipline to choose depth over immediacy.

And perhaps most important of all, discipline to stay true to your core signal, even as the ecosystem around you shifts.

Because it will shift, algorithms will change. Formats will evolve. Platforms will rise and fall. But a signal, precise, resonant, repeatable, will outlast all of it. The internet will always have room for people who know what they're saying, say it well, and say it often enough to become real in the minds of others.

And so you arrive at a new posture. No longer shouting into the void and no longer hoping to be found. You become the steady pulse around which others begin to organize their thinking. You become part of how they understand the space, the conversation, even themselves. You go from being one voice among many to a voice that matters.

This is the work of a signal.

It is not glamorous. It is not always fast.

But it is the most durable form of digital leverage available to anyone willing to build with intention.

In the chapters ahead, we'll look at the platforms themselves, not from a tactical checklist perspective, but from the angle of power, patterns, and positioning. We will explore what each platform rewards, how it perceives identity, and how to train it to surface you again and again. But you now understand the foundation. Without a signal, no amount of strategy can hold. With a signal, almost anything you do becomes easier.

This chapter has not been about metrics. It's been about meaning. Because in the end, the feed is just a machine. What it elevates is a reflection of what it's been taught to value. And what it values most is a signal that doesn't blur. Signal that stays sharp, even when the noise grows louder.

That signal, if you build it carefully, can last longer than the platform that delivers it.

Chapter Four: Platforms as Ecosystems

There is a fundamental misunderstanding that dominates the way most people approach social platforms. They see them as distribution tools, places to push content, to get attention, to "go viral." But platforms are not passive channels. They are not digital billboards or sterile arenas awaiting your brilliance. Platforms are ecosystems. And like all ecosystems, they have rules, flows, and invisible forces that shape behavior in ways most users never fully see.

To operate effectively within these environments, you must stop thinking like a user and begin thinking like an ecosystem navigator. That shift may sound abstract, but it changes everything. Because once you understand a platform not as a thing to use, but as a dynamic organism to participate in, your strategy transforms. You no longer ask, "How do I get more likes?" You ask, "What kind of energy thrives here, and how do I channel mine into something the system wants to amplify?"

This isn't about gaming the system. It's about aligning your signal with the underlying flows of each digital environment. Because every platform has a different set of incentives baked into its structure, and those incentives shape not only what content performs, but what kind of person the platform favors.

Let's take LinkedIn, for instance. On the surface, it appears to reward expertise. But underneath, it rewards clarity, confidence, and narrative. The best-performing content is rarely the most technical; it's the most *relatable with authority*. The platform's feed is engineered to boost posts that are easy to skim, fast to engage with, and capable of sparking emotional agreement without appearing polarizing. It's a business platform, yes, but it's also a stage for storytelling. The person who masters that dual identity, both credible and human, becomes magnetic.

Contrast that with Twitter (or X, depending on your preference), which operates more like a neural network than a feed. Here, the game is speed and sharpness. The algorithm is attuned to frequency, interaction density, and the ability to spawn second-order conversations. Authority matters, but it's often earned through wit, clarity, and reaction time rather than credentials. Twitter rewards the person who can distill a worldview into a sentence, and do so in real time, in front of an audience that has no patience for fluff.

Then there's Instagram, a platform long dominated by aesthetics but now fragmented into competing modes: image, story, and reel. Each mode caters to a different attention behavior. Static image posts are largely nostalgic now, a throwback to the early 2010s. Stories operate like ephemeral diaries, designed for intimacy. Reels are the current engine, fueled by audio, movement, and immediacy. The platform as a whole is emotionally driven, and while it's possible to build thought leadership here, it must be layered over visual presence. On Instagram, value is filtered through *vibe*, and if your vibe doesn't match the mood of the medium, your ideas won't travel.

YouTube operates more like a slow-burning archive than a social feed. Its searchability and long-tail structure favor creators who play the long game. Videos that gain traction often do so over months, not hours. This rewards depth, intentionality, and a degree of production quality that signals care. Unlike other platforms, where your best work can vanish in 24 hours,

YouTube holds memory. It's the platform where signals can compound in public, and the audience it attracts is often more invested, more deliberate in their consumption.

Even newer or niche platforms like TikTok or Substack carry distinct environmental cues. TikTok is an algorithm-first environment where follower count matters less than individual post performance. It rewards risk, experimentation, and personality. Substack, meanwhile, is slow media. It invites readers who want to dwell, not scroll. It favors writers who build a relationship with their audience over time, through rhythm, insight, and voice rather than spectacle.

The point isn't to master all of these at once. It's essential to understand that every platform is an attention ecosystem with its unique climate. The soil that nourishes a creator on one may suffocate them on another. The skill isn't just in being a good communicator; it's in knowing how to shape your communication so it can survive and thrive in different digital habitats.

You cannot post the same way everywhere and expect resonance. That's not because your ideas aren't good; it's because you haven't translated them into the local language of the platform. The ecosystem doesn't reject you. It simply doesn't recognize you as native.

Think of this like biodiversity. A signal that thrives in one ecosystem, dense, long-form, context-rich, may die in another that favors brevity, momentum, or aesthetic punch. The creator who tries to copy and paste content across channels will always feel like they're spinning their wheels. The one who adapts, who remixes rather than replicates, begins to move with the current instead of against it.

But adaptation doesn't mean compromise. You don't need to dilute your voice. You need to *translate* it. That's what ecosystem thinking allows you to do. It provides a framework for aligning your content with each platform's attention dynamics, without compromising the integrity of your signal. This is the beginning of strategic presence, not just showing up everywhere, but showing up differently where it counts.

As you begin to engage with platforms through the lens of ecosystems, you start to notice that each one also creates its type of identity. That identity isn't something you explicitly choose; it's something the system infers from your behavior. What you post, how often, what people engage with, and what they ignore, all of it trains the machine to understand who you are, whether you intended it or not.

This is why inconsistency doesn't just make you harder to follow; it makes you more challenging to find. The algorithm learns from repetition, not intent. It doesn't know what you meant to become. It only knows what you've taught it to expect. And if what you teach changes every week, the signal it sends back to the feed is uncertainty. Uncertainty doesn't just confuse the machine; it weakens your gravity. You become another blur in the scroll.

To avoid that fate, you have to become deliberate not just about what you post, but about how your body of work forms an arc. That arc doesn't have to be linear or even planned. But it must be coherent. Each post should feel like part of a larger constellation. Not because you've locked yourself into a narrow niche, but because you've curated a lens, something recognizable in tone, structure, or energy. This is how you become a shape in the system, rather than a flicker.

This shaping isn't a one-time decision. It's a recursive act. You post, you observe, you adjust. Not based solely on performance metrics, but on alignment, does this piece reflect what you want to be known for? Does it fit the ecosystem you're trying to grow within? Does it serve the audience you are intentionally attracting, rather than a transient burst of strangers who may never return?

Most creators never make this leap. They build their presence reactively, chasing what's working now, rather than shaping what could work repeatedly. They confuse spikes with success. They confuse reach with recognition. And in doing so, they surrender their strategy to platform volatility. The result is a cycle of frustration: a few posts go wide, engagement surges, then collapses. They try to replicate the high, but the energy's gone. The feed moves on. They start over.

This isn't failure, it's friction. And friction is what you eliminate when you build with an ecosystem mindset.

Because here's the truth: each platform has a rhythm. Some are fast and relentless. Others are slow and cumulative. Some reward commentary. Others reward curation. Some lift voices that entertain. Others elevate those who educate. These rhythms are not obvious when you're just consuming. They only become clear when you begin to operate from a higher altitude, seeing not just content, but currents.

Once you see those currents, you can begin to align your efforts with the momentum already present in the platform. On Twitter, this might mean injecting your voice into emergent conversations in real time, rather than waiting to polish a perfect thread. On LinkedIn, it might mean structuring your insights into stories and mini-essays, designed to trigger comment chains and algorithmic reinforcement. On Instagram, it could mean packaging your ideas into visual metaphors or reel formats that echo what's currently trending, but subtly reframe them through your lens.

It's a dance between mimicry and originality. Too much mimicry, and you vanish into the noise. Too much originality without format awareness, and you remain invisible. The sweet spot is knowing the choreography well enough to move with style, to echo the rhythm of the platform without becoming generic.

And that requires paying attention to more than your output. It requires studying the environment to notice what kinds of creators are gaining traction and why—watching how ideas travel. Observing what gets shared, what gets saved, and what gets ignored. And then stepping back to ask: how do I express my signal in a way that this particular ecosystem can recognize and reward?

This approach isn't flashy. It won't give you a ten-step content calendar or a cheat code for instant virality. But what it will provide you with is adaptive intelligence, the ability to modulate your expression without compromising your identity. And that intelligence is what creates resilience. Platforms change. Incentives evolve. But those who know how to read the room and speak its language don't just survive the shifts. They capitalize on them.

This is especially true when you begin to scale across multiple platforms. Many creators make the mistake of trying to grow everywhere at once, copying content from one place to another without understanding the expectations of each. What results is a diluted presence, half-formed on every platform, full-bodied on none. A better strategy is to go deep before you go wide—master one ecosystem. Build resonance. Understand its rules. Then, and only then, begin to adapt your signal for others.

When you do, you'll find that certain elements translate naturally. Your voice, core themes, and worldview can travel. But the container must shift. What works as a tweet may require a full carousel on Instagram. What earns clicks on YouTube may need to be distilled into a single insight for LinkedIn. Your essence stays the same. Your expression becomes elastic.

This elasticity is a strategic asset. It allows you to expand without fracturing. It will enable you to show up in multiple spaces without splintering your identity. And most importantly, it will allow your audience to recognize you across contexts, not because you're everywhere, but because you are unmistakably yourself wherever you appear.

That is what it means to be platform-agnostic without being identity-neutral.

And in a world where audiences are fragmented, feeds are fickle, and formats evolve monthly, this kind of presence becomes a competitive advantage.

You're not just playing the game.

You're shaping the field.

When you start to see platforms as living systems, each with its own rules, rhythms, and evolutionary traits, it becomes clear that the work of visibility is less about force and more about fit. You're not pushing your content uphill, hoping something catches. You're shaping it to flow with the terrain, carving a channel that the algorithm can fill again and again with new attention. And this only works if you understand that your presence on any given platform is not a performance, it's a negotiation.

Every time you publish, you are negotiating with an invisible logic. You are offering your signal in exchange for distribution. And that distribution is not based on merit in a vacuum. It is based on whether your post fits the current moment, the platform's internal logic, and the behavior patterns of the people using it right now. You may have something brilliant to say, but if it's structured in a way that feels alien to the ecosystem, it won't be heard. Not because it isn't worthy, but because the system doesn't know where to place it.

This is where so many thoughtful creators get stuck. They believe that quality alone should surface. They pour time and care into their work, polishing every sentence and sharpening every insight. But their structure doesn't match the context. Their post reads like a long-form essay in a space built for bursts. Or it speaks in nuance to an audience looking for clarity. Or it lands without energy in a feed that rewards intensity. The message might be right. But the vessel is wrong.

Matching the vessel to the message is not a compromise; it's a strategy. It's understanding that attention is not just earned, it's translated. It's not enough to say something valuable. You must express it in a way that the platform supports and the audience can comprehend. That's what makes content spread. Not tricks. Not gimmicks. Not conformity. Translation.

And translation begins with awareness.

Awareness of the platform. Of its design, its culture, its dominant formats. Awareness of your audience, not as abstract demographics, but as real people with rhythms, expectations, and emotional bandwidth. And understanding of yourself, your voice, your ideas, your core message that shouldn't shift, even as your methods do.

When you develop that kind of awareness, your presence becomes multidimensional. You stop being reactive. You start being adaptive. You notice shifts before they become crashes. You see opportunity not just in trends, but in absences, those quiet gaps in the ecosystem where your voice can emerge as something fresh.

This is what separates those who play the game for a moment from those who redefine it over time.

The long-term creators, the ones who aren't just relevant now but will be relevant a decade from now, understand ecosystems intimately. They know which formats to favor, which conversations to join, and which patterns to break. They know how to shape their presence not to fit in, but to resonate. And when they expand to new platforms, they don't start over. They scale. Because their signal isn't bound to a feed, it's embedded in how they think, speak, and show up.

This is the highest form of algorithmic leverage: not hacking the system but training it to recognize your signal across contexts. When the machine learns that your presence generates time-on-site, meaningful interaction, or user retention, it begins to surface you more often. Not because you gamed it, but because you gave it what it wanted in a way only you can deliver.

But you must never forget that this is still a negotiation. And negotiations can change.

The platform may shift its incentives. Your audience may mature. The culture may pivot. And when that happens, the creators who rely only on tactics will scramble. The ones who understand ecosystems will adjust. Not reactively, but deliberately. They'll pause, observe, recalibrate, and realign. They'll find the new flow. Because their strategy isn't built on the feed, it's built on understanding.

And that understanding gives you one thing most creators never have: durability.

Durability is not built on trends. It's built on patterns. On depth. On the ability to survive algorithm shifts not by luck, but by design. A durable creator doesn't fear platform change. They expect it. And when it comes, they don't panic. They adapt with clarity because they've built something more profound than a content calendar. They've built a system of expression that can bend without a Master.

That system begins with a signal. It grows with structure. And it comes to life through alignment with the ecosystem.

Which brings us to the next part of the puzzle: how do you turn that system into something that lasts? Not just into momentum, but into identity? How do you become more than a creator with posts, but a presence that matters over time?

That's the work of narrative.

Because even the most consistent signal, delivered in the most platform-optimized structure, can only go so far without a deeper arc. People don't just follow ideas. They follow stories. And when your work begins to feel like a story unfolding, when your presence starts to suggest movement, intention, and growth, your audience stops consuming you and starts investing in you.

That's when things change.

In the next chapter, we'll explore this in detail, how to construct narrative arcs that don't just entertain, but also anchor. We'll look at how to sequence your content in ways that build emotional continuity, strategic positioning, and long-term trust. Because when content is episodic, when ideas are layered, when presence becomes plot, that's when attention turns into allegiance.

And allegiance, once earned, is more powerful than any algorithm.

Chapter Five: Narrative Power

Attention gets you noticed. Signal keeps you consistent. Ecosystem fluency helps you grow. But if your goal is to transcend the volatility of the feed, to become more than an occasional flash and instead emerge as a fixture in the minds of your audience, then you need narrative. Not marketing narrative. Not fabricated origin stories or buzzword-laden positioning decks. You need *authentic narrative power*: the capacity to create continuity between moments, to turn fragments into arcs, and to make your presence feel like a journey worth following.

Narrative isn't what you say in one post. It's what your body of work implies over time. It's the connective tissue between your insights, your experiences, your stances. And it's what makes people feel like they're not just reading your ideas, but traveling with you, seeing your perspective evolve, your language sharpen, your convictions deepen.

The mistake many creators make is assuming narrative is a luxury, something reserved for authors, filmmakers, or keynote speakers. But in a world of fractured attention, narrative is a necessity. It's what transforms a disjointed sequence of posts into something cohesive. It's what gives your work emotional weight. It's what turns silent lurkers into invested followers. Not because you entertained them, but because you made them feel part of something.

Narrative begins with direction. Not necessarily a rigid plan or defined endpoint, but a sense that your work is going *somewhere*. People want to feel like they're watching a progression, not a repetition of the same post in different outfits, but an unfolding.

This doesn't mean you must constantly reinvent yourself. The best narratives often evolve around a fixed center. The creator holds a core belief or question steady, and what changes is the way they explore it, apply it, or challenge it over time.

That evolution is what builds trust. When your audience sees that you are not just regurgitating slogans but thinking in public, iterating, confronting your own biases, adjusting your stance with integrity, they start to believe in the integrity of your voice. They see you as a human mind in motion, not a content machine. And that's rare enough to be magnetic.

But narrative is not just internal. It's also structural. It shows up in how you sequence your work. Are your posts building on each other, or contradicting each other? Are you revisiting themes in a way that deepens their meaning, or simply reusing them? Are you layering your signal across formats, perhaps expanding on something in a newsletter that began as a thread, or using a podcast to explore what a tweet merely hinted at?

These acts of layering don't require dramatic effort. They require intentionality. They require asking not just, "What do I want to say today?" but "Where does this idea live within the larger arc of what I'm building?"

Think of your work not as content but as chapters. Not in the literal sense of organizing them as a book, but in the sense that each new post, essay, or appearance contributes to the unfolding of a bigger story. A story about your domain, your expertise, your values, and your audience's role within it.

Because here's the quiet truth about narrative power: it isn't only about you. The strongest narratives are those that invite participation. When people follow you, they aren't just consuming your journey. They are mapping themselves into it. They are identifying with your struggles, applying your insights, and echoing your ideas in their work. You become a proxy for a future version of themselves. And once that identification happens, the bond becomes emotional, not just informational.

That's what makes narrative sticky. It's not about attention anymore. It's about alignment.

And alignment is where leverage lives.

Platforms do not grant leverage. People grant it. And people grant it when they believe you are not just interesting but *accurate*, when your arc makes sense, when your contradictions are thoughtful rather than erratic, and when your presence helps them locate or refine something in their own lives.

This is why narrative power cannot be faked. You can hire a brand strategist. You can write an origin story. But if your output doesn't reflect continuity, coherence, and growth, the audience will feel the gap. They may not be able to articulate it, but they'll sense that something isn't real. And in an age where performance is everywhere, the rarest currency is believability.

Believability isn't about perfection. It's about consistency, not just in message, but in evolution. Your audience doesn't need you to be certain. They need you to be *in motion*. That motion is what gives your ideas momentum. It's what turns "here's a thought" into "here's someone I want to learn from over time."

To wield narrative power, then, you must begin to track your arc. Not performatively. Internally. Ask yourself: What am I exploring? What questions keep resurfacing in my work? What has changed in my thinking over the past year? What parts of my past am I still integrating? What do I now reject that I once embraced?

These questions are not for content. They are for orientation. Because when you understand your arc, you start to speak from the center of it. And from that center, your voice becomes stable, even when the world shifts around you.

When creators ignore the importance of narrative, they often fall into the trap of episodic brilliance. A post here, a clever idea there, sometimes even a viral moment. But without a narrative thread pulling it all together, these bursts of insight float in isolation. The audience may enjoy them in the moment, but the impression fades. The creator becomes a random source of noise, not a signal to follow. They are remembered vaguely, if at all.

Narrative changes this. It gives the audience a reason to return. It creates a trail, a breadcrumb path that leads somewhere. And even more importantly, it trains the audience to expect growth. That expectation is crucial. Because when someone believes that following you means becoming smarter, more aware, more articulate, or more connected, they invest more of themselves into your journey.

This is where narrative power merges with psychological positioning. You are not simply presenting information. You are shaping an identity, for yourself, yes, but also for the audience member who follows you. When you show your work evolving, you implicitly invite your followers to do the same. When you reveal your thought process, not just the finished idea, but the path you took to arrive at it, you help them locate their process. Your voice becomes a mirror, and over time, that mirroring creates loyalty that metrics alone cannot measure.

You might be wondering: what does narrative look like in practice, especially in environments that reward short-form content, reactive posting, and instant feedback? It seems like thematic recurrence. It looks like returning to foundational questions, not with redundancy, but with a new perspective. It looks like referencing your past work, not to boast, but to show a throughline. It appears that articulating how your current insight relates to a broader set of ideas you've explored before is key. These narrative gestures don't have to be overt. They can be subtle. A familiar phrase. A callback to a metaphor. A shift in tone that signals change. Over time, they create a sense of continuity, which in turn builds emotional equity.

This is especially important in a landscape where so much content is forgettable. People are drowning in posts. What they remember, what sticks, are the voices that feel grounded. That carries an internal rhythm. That seems to be going somewhere. Not faster, not louder, just deeper. A creator with narrative power can whisper and still be heard because their audience has been trained to listen closely.

And here's the deeper magic: narrative builds reputation, even when you're not posting. When your body of work holds together, when your ideas echo across time, people begin to reference you even in your absence. Your presence remains alive in conversations you aren't in. Your content circulates not because it's recent, but because it's resonant. And that resonance is the narrative's long tail. It creates visibility that survives platform shifts, algorithmic changes, and even your seasons of silence.

This isn't a romantic idea; it's strategic positioning. Most creators burn out because they believe consistency means constant output. They think that if they stop posting, they'll disappear. But when you build through narrative, your ideas keep working even when you're not. The arc does the work. The storyline sustains momentum. The audience carries the conversation forward because they feel part of something that lives beyond any single post.

To get there, you need to start thinking in arcs. Not grand, sweeping narratives that require years to unfold. Just enough structure to create movement. Maybe it's a three-part breakdown of a complex idea, delivered over a week. Perhaps it's a monthly theme that anchors your thinking and signals to your audience what you're exploring now. Maybe it's a series that traces how your views on a topic have changed. Whatever the shape, the goal is to move from isolated moments to layered continuity.

That continuity doesn't require elaborate planning. What it needs is reflection—noticing your patterns and seeing where ideas repeat, where they shift, where they challenge each other. Then, using those shifts as narrative energy. Letting your work not just inform, but transform, first you, then your readers.

It also means embracing your contradictions. Too many creators strive for a kind of sterile consistency, afraid that change will be seen as weakness or inconsistency. But real narrative power lies in the ability to grow in public without losing trust. To say, "I used to think this. Now I see it differently." Not as a brand pivot, but as an honest reflection of intellectual and emotional evolution.

Audiences respect that. More than that, they crave it. They are starving for voices that model nuance, complexity, and growth. In a world of hot takes and rigid binaries, a creator who can hold tension, who can evolve their thinking without discarding their identity, becomes a rare and valuable presence.

Narrative is how you demonstrate that ability. Not by stating it, but by embodying it. Over time. In full view. With all the risk and honesty that entails.

And here's what happens when you do: your audience not only follows you, but they defend you. They advocate for you. They reference your work when it's relevant. They link back to posts from months ago. They connect dots across your timeline. Because they aren't just consuming your content, they're participating in your growth.

This is what turns a feed into a following. What turns attention into allegiance.

And what turns a creator into a voice that outlives the platform?

If you've ever wondered why some creators remain visible long after their output slows, it's because their narrative has taken root in the minds of others. Their voice continues to echo, not because of algorithmic favor or paid promotion, but because they've built a story people want to keep following. Even in their absence, the arc continues. It's as if the audience is holding their place in the feed, waiting for the next chapter.

This is not mysticism. It's architecture. Narrative power is built the way cathedrals are built, stone by stone, not in haste, but with deliberate placement, an awareness of form, and a respect for time. Each idea you share becomes a structural element. Alone, it may be just another piece of content. But when assembled with care, it contributes to something far greater: a shape that others can move through, learn from, and return to.

What's required, though, is discipline, not the kind tied to productivity hacks, but a deeper kind of attentiveness. You must be willing to see your work as part of a larger structure, not a series of disconnected acts. You must treat your ideas as if they matter beyond the scroll. That mindset won't earn instant metrics. But it will earn legacy. And in the long game of digital presence, issues of legacy far outweigh virality.

Think of the creators whose work has shaped your thinking, not those who merely entertained you, but those who rearranged something in you. Chances are, they didn't just post well. They told a story. About who they were. About what they believed. About what was possible. And they did so with enough persistence and precision that you began to see the world differently because of them.

That is the power you hold, too, if you choose to use narrative as more than decoration.

The most effective use of narrative isn't just to build audience affinity. The goal is to create a long-term framework for self-alignment. When you know your arc, when you've defined the central questions you're working through, the values you're clarifying, the ideas you're shaping, every creative decision becomes easier. What to post. What to write. What to say no to. Narrative becomes your filter, not just your amplifier.

It also becomes your protection. In the era of constant content, it's easy to get pulled off course. Chasing engagement. Mimicking competitors. Reacting to trends. Narrative anchors you. It reminds you why you started, and what you're building toward. It keeps you from mistaking noise for opportunity. And it offers you a structure for recovering when you lose your way.

That structure doesn't have to be rigid. The best narrative arcs leave room for surprise, for chapters you didn't see coming, for insights that emerge from lived experience rather than planned campaigns. But even within that openness, there's direction. There's momentum. There's a sense that you're not just reacting to the feed, you're composing a larger work, one installment at a time.

And that's what distinguishes a presence from a personality. Personalities are curated, optimized, carefully maintained, but ultimately interchangeable. Presence is different. Presence carries weight. It's not built on charisma. It's built on continuity. The sense that something deeper is happening, and that by following you, others get to witness and participate in that unfolding.

This is what people are looking for, whether they can articulate it or not. Not just content that informs or entertains, but content that means something. Content that fits into a bigger picture. Content that helps them feel like they are on a path, not just in a scroll.

When your work begins to offer that kind of meaning, everything changes. You stop fighting for every ounce of engagement. You stop second-guessing every post. You stop burning out from the constant pressure to produce. Because your presence starts to work on its own. The arc begins to carry. The story starts to compound. And the people who are meant to follow you begin to find you, not because you reached them, but because your signal, layered in narrative, pulled them in.

This isn't theoretical. It's structural. And it's available to anyone willing to think beyond the moment and begin constructing meaning across time.

Narrative power is not a strategy. It's a stance.

A stance of continuity in a world obsessed with novelty.

A stance of intention in a culture driven by reaction.

A stance of evolution in a system that rewards repetition.

And above all, a stance of authorship, of refusing to let the platform write your story for you.

Because once you own the narrative, you change your position in the system. You're no longer trying to be seen. You're creating a world people want to enter.

And from there, everything you publish becomes more than content.

It becomes part of a canon.

Chapter Six: Compounding Presence

There is a quiet shift that occurs in the life of a creator when they cross the threshold from temporary visibility into lasting presence. At first, the work is manual. Each post must push through noise. Each interaction feels earned through effort. There is momentum, but no inertia. Your output exists in isolation, like stones dropped into a deep lake, making ripples, yes, but fading fast unless the next is already prepared. But over time, something begins to change. A current develops. Your ideas start to echo even when you're silent. Others quote you without prompting. Opportunities arrive without outreach. This is the onset of compounding presence.

Unlike virality, which is explosive and unpredictable, compounding presence is slow and deliberate. It builds not through bursts, but through layers. It does not depend on gimmicks or tactics, but on the steady accumulation of resonance. Each insight, each articulation, each moment of clarity adds to a body of work that eventually begins to carry weight independent of platform algorithms or short-term trends. It becomes a living archive, an ecosystem of thought that others can move through, reference, and return to over time.

What's essential to understand about compounding presence is that it is not merely a function of volume. Posting more often does not, in itself, guarantee depth. Output without intention can dilute presence rather than amplify it. The difference lies in coherence. Compounding occurs when your work consistently reinforces a set of core ideas, a voice, a worldview. When those elements align, each new piece doesn't just exist; it connects. It references the past, expands the present, and makes room for the future.

This kind of coherence does not mean rigidity. It doesn't require that you speak about the same topics forever. What it needs is thematic integrity. Your ideas can evolve. Your style can shift. Your interests can widen. But there must remain a traceable thread, a sense that this is still you speaking, still you thinking, still you unfolding in public. Without that thread, your work becomes fragmented. With it, you begin to generate gravity.

Gravity is what keeps people close, even when you go quiet. It's what causes your audience to scroll through your archives, to seek out your older pieces, to feel that engaging with your content is part of something larger than entertainment. That gravity deepens when your presence feels durable, not because you're always online, but because your body of work holds together, even in your absence. People trust that when you speak, it's worth listening to. They give you the benefit of the doubt, the gift of patience. And in a world built on instant reaction, that kind of trust is rare.

Trust, however, is not granted lightly. It is earned through consistency, not just in frequency, but in substance. If your audience senses that you're showing up with something to say, not just something to sell, they stay. If they feel you respect their time, their attention, and their intelligence, they begin to invest. That investment doesn't always look like a comment or a share. Sometimes it looks like silence, a person thinking about your post hours later, referencing your words in a meeting, or changing their behavior in subtle ways because of something you've articulated.

These invisible effects are the true markers of compounding. They cannot be tracked on a dashboard. But over time, they create a presence that platforms respond to. Not because you're feeding the algorithm with content volume, but because users are signaling that your presence is valuable. They spend more time on your posts. They click through more of your work. They return. The platform learns to prioritize your signal not through tricks, but through genuine engagement.

This is why compounding presence requires patience. You will not see exponential growth in the beginning. The early stages may feel slow, even punishing. But what's happening is foundational. You are teaching the system and your audience how to interpret your signal. You are laying the groundwork for a presence that, once established, becomes self-sustaining. The work you do today may not pay off this week, but if constructed with care, it will pay off repeatedly over time.

To build that kind of system, you must treat your content not as discrete events, but as assets. Assets have longevity. They are crafted for endurance, not just impact. An asset is a piece of work that continues to serve your presence long after the metrics fade. It might be a powerful essay that others reference for years. A foundational thread that defines your philosophy. A video that lives in the search archive and continues to bring in new minds. These assets are the cornerstones of your compounding effect.

You don't need many. A few, done well, can anchor an entire digital presence. But they must be constructed with a different mindset and not rushed. Not reactive. Not built to meet a deadline or post quota. Built with an eye toward clarity, resonance, and timelessness. The kind of content that could be rediscovered months or years later and still feel vital.

This is not glamorous work. It requires turning down the volume on trend-chasing. It requires resisting the pressure always to be immediate. But the long-term payoff is substantial. Because once these assets are in place, your content engine begins to shift from push to pull. Instead of constantly having to remind people you exist, they begin to seek you out. You move from the periphery of their attention to something closer to their center of gravity.

And once you occupy that kind of position, you are no longer dependent on platform whims. You become, in effect, algorithm-proof, not because the algorithm no longer matters, but because your presence has become powerful enough to move through any environment with momentum intact.

To reach the point where your digital presence compounds naturally, you must understand that it is not a function of platform mastery alone. It's about becoming structurally relevant, building a reputation for consistency of value, not just consistency of posting. That distinction matters. The internet is littered with creators who post daily yet leave no lasting trace. They fill the feed but leave no impression. Their names fade with the scroll, their voices blending into the ambient noise of online production.

Contrast that with someone whose name surfaces regularly in discussions they're not even part of. Their past work continues to be referenced. Their ideas show up in boardrooms, internal documents, or strategy decks, even if those ideas were first shared in a casual Twitter thread. That's the quiet force of compounded narrative and strategic presence. Their influence is no longer tied to a timestamp. It exists independently of freshness. Its relevance without recency.

That state is earned by creating what could be called intellectual infrastructure. These are the recurring, recognizable structures in your body of work, concepts, phrases, metaphors, or arguments that your audience begins to associate with you. Not because you've claimed ownership, but because you've clarified the idea with such precision that others remember you in connection with it. This might be a mental model you developed. It might be a method you named. It might be a metaphor you popularized. What matters is not just the originality, but the repetition across contexts. You become known not only for what you say, but for the shape of your thinking.

Creators who build this kind of infrastructure are playing a different game. They are not simply publishing to perform; they are publishing to construct. They are laying track in front of themselves, building a system that others can enter and explore. That exploration deepens the audience relationship far beyond a casual follow. It creates intellectual loyalty, a sense that engaging with your work is not just informative, but foundational.

This loyalty is subtle at first. It may not show up in likes or shares. But it appears in other ways. People start to cite you without tagging you. They reference your frameworks in private. They teach others using your language. When you release something new, it gets attention not because it's promoted heavily, but because it fits into an arc the audience is already tracking. They don't need to be convinced. They're already invested.

This is the natural outcome of the presence of compounds. Each piece you publish adds weight to the whole. Each iteration reinforces your voice. Each expansion of an idea strengthens the foundation. Eventually, your presence becomes a kind of terrain in its own right, something others move through, build upon, or navigate with. And at that point, your visibility is no longer fragile. It's fortified.

But to reach that point, you must resist the urge to chase every opportunity that crosses your feed. Compounding presence demands selectivity. Not every trend deserves your attention. Not every prompt merits a response. The temptation to insert yourself into every conversation is strong, especially in an environment where visibility feels like survival. But over-participation dilutes positioning. When you comment on everything, your point of view starts to blur. You become a commentator, not a creator. You react, rather than shape.

There is a discipline in saying less but saying it better. There is power in letting silence work in your favor, allowing gaps between your outputs to build anticipation rather than suspicion. In a culture obsessed with speed, intentional pacing can become a signature. When your audience knows that you won't flood them with noise, they start to lean in when you speak. And that lean-in is worth more than a hundred casual views.

Presence compounds most powerfully when paired with scarcity. Not scarcity of value, but shortage of voice. You are available but not overexposed. You are consistent, but not redundant. Your ideas reappear in the culture, not because you push them endlessly, but because they are worth repeating. This kind of restraint is challenging to master. It goes against every instinct the algorithm cultivates. But it is essential for long-term differentiation.

Creators who understand this begin to approach their work differently. They stop asking what will go viral. They start asking what will be helpful in five years. They measure success not in engagement spikes but in the quality of attention they hold. They think in terms of resonance, not just reach. They trade short-term metrics for long-term memory.

And perhaps most critically, they begin to build with legacy in mind, not in the grandiose, self-important sense of becoming a "thought leader," but in the grounded recognition that work worth doing should be designed to last. That each piece of content is not just a unit of attention, it is a building block in something more enduring. An idea ecosystem. A digital canon. A presence that can outlive the platforms it lives on.

This shift doesn't happen all at once. It emerges slowly, through deliberate iteration and reflection. Through the decision to treat your work not just as output, but as a form of authorship. By recognizing that you are not just trying to be seen, you're laying the groundwork for others to build upon.

Once you internalize that, your relationship with content changes. You stop obsessing over performance and start focusing on structure. You stop seeking validation and start constructing value. And over time, that shift in orientation builds something that no algorithm can take away.

A presence that generates its momentum.

One of the less discussed, but most consequential outcomes of compounding presence is that it alters your relationship to the very platforms that once dictated your visibility. In the early stages of growth, you are bound to them. Every impression feels earned through careful compliance, posting at the correct times, optimizing for engagement, and adhering to the shifting etiquette of the feed. You are, in effect, an operator inside someone else's machine. But as your presence compounds, that balance begins to shift. You become less reactive to the platform and more generative within it.

This isn't about control in the traditional sense. No one controls the algorithm. But compounding presence means your ideas begin to develop their internal logic. People start to find you not through tags or shares, but through reputation, through recommendation, through the echo effect of consistent relevance. At a certain point, people aren't just interacting with your latest post; they're exploring your archive. They're reading your work not because it's trending, but because it has accumulated the kind of depth that invites repeated attention.

This is when the shift becomes irreversible. The platforms that once constrained you now begin to mirror your patterns. The algorithm, which rewards engagement and retention, recognizes that your audience lingers. That they return. That they click through, share, save, or open more than average. These quiet signals teach the system that your content is not just momentarily interesting but structurally valuable—and so your visibility increases, not in explosive spikes, but in steady elevation. The floor rises. Your baseline reach grows. You are no longer fighting for scraps of attention. You have built a presence that the system begins to recognize and surface because it serves the system's interests.

Yet the valid reward of compounding isn't algorithmic. It's existential. You no longer live in fear of disappearance. You no longer wake up wondering what to post to stay visible. You have created a space, mental, intellectual, and emotional, where you are allowed to think. You are allowed to pause. You are allowed to develop without panic. The content treadmill becomes the cadence of your design. And in that space, you can do your best work.

This shift changes how you make decisions. Instead of chasing relevance, you begin to pursue resonance. Instead of crafting your ideas to be consumed quickly, you shape them to be remembered. You stop trying to "go viral," not because virality is bad, but because you understand it's unpredictable and often unsustainable. What you seek instead is significance, work that holds its shape long after the scroll has passed.

Creators who reach this level often become stewards of their domain. They are no longer voices in a feed; they are reference points. Others in their field begin to cite them without prompting. New entrants use their language as shorthand. Their work shapes conversations they're not even part of, and their name carries a weight that cannot be measured by followers alone.

To be clear, this kind of presence does not require fame. It requires a foundation. You do not need millions of followers. You need a body of work that coheres. A perspective that holds. A narrative that deepens. An audience that listens. With those elements in place, your impact compounds, not because of scale, but because of clarity.

That clarity allows you to weather volatility. Algorithm changes. Audience churn. Platform decay. When others are panicking about decreased reach or shifting incentives, you adjust, but you do not flail. You revisit your foundations. You reconnect with your narrative. You continue your arc. Because you are not here to win a trend. You are here to build a presence that matters across time.

This is the ultimate irony of compounding presence. It looks effortless from the outside. People assume that your visibility comes easily, that your ideas land with impact because you're lucky or well-connected. But what they don't see is the years of alignment that made it possible. The consistency of voice. The discipline of thought. The refusal to chase novelty at the expense of integrity. The silent days spent refining an idea that would only be shared when ready, not when the calendar demanded it.

These invisible choices are the scaffolding of presence. They are the difference between relevance and durability.

Durability is what allows you to remain, to evolve, to continue speaking with clarity even as the landscape shifts. It is what turns your digital presence from a series of posts into a meaningful body of work. And in a world addicted to immediacy, there is perhaps no greater act of resistance, and no greater source of leverage, than building something that lasts.

So if your goal is not just to be seen today, but to matter tomorrow, then compounding presence is not optional. It is the path. It is the quiet accumulation of coherence, trust, narrative, and clarity over time. And while it may not grant you instant visibility, it grants you something infinitely more valuable: the ability to shape culture from the inside out.

When you build that kind of presence, the system begins to adapt to you. Your voice becomes infrastructure. Your perspective becomes orientation. And your body of work becomes a place others go to remember what matters.

That is what it means to break the algorithm, not by beating it at its own game, but by building something so compelling, so coherent, so unshakably grounded that it no longer matters who controls the feed.

You are no longer part of the noise. You are the signal.

Chapter Seven: Trust as Leverage

For all the talk about metrics, reach, impressions, and engagement rates, there remains one force that quietly determines whether any of it translates into real influence, sustained visibility, or the ability to shape behavior: trust. Not the trust of platforms or algorithms, but the trust of actual people. The kind of trust that isn't declared with a like or rewarded with a share, but that lives beneath the surface, guiding decisions and anchoring relationships over time.

It is a strange thing, how rarely trust is discussed in strategic terms, especially in the digital space where its absence is everywhere. Audiences are skeptical, even cynical, and often with good reason. They have been sold under the guise of authenticity, manipulated by clickbait disguised as expertise, and drawn in by charisma, only to be disappointed by inconsistency. Over time, they have developed defenses, mental filters that sort the sincere from the performative in milliseconds. And into this gauntlet steps anyone attempting to grow a presence online.

The assumption that trust can be assumed is perhaps the most significant strategic error a creator or founder can make. Trust is not the default. It is not the starting point. Credentials, charisma, or production quality do not guarantee it. Trust is built, brick by brick, over time, through signals that accumulate into belief. And when it is absent, even the most technically flawless content struggles to land. Without trust, there is no weight. Without trust, there is no leverage.

Leverage, in this context, is not about power over others. It's about permission. It's about the freedom to speak longer, to speak deeper, to offer nuance instead of noise. When your audience trusts you, you don't need to grab attention with cheap tricks. You already have it. You don't need to persuade with urgency. Your readers arrive predisposed to consider. You don't have to fight for visibility. People carry your voice with them and surface it when it's needed most.

This kind of leverage is rare because it cannot be faked. It cannot be purchased. It must be earned through sustained integrity. And that integrity shows up in ways that are often invisible to the casual observer. It's in the consistency of your tone, the coherence of your message, the humility with which you handle critique, the thoughtfulness of your replies, and the rhythm of your presence over time. These are not flashy behaviors. They don't produce viral spikes. But they create a subterranean structure of credibility that platforms eventually reward, and that people feel long before they articulate it.

Trust begins with clarity. If your message is inconsistent, if your positioning shifts with every trend, if your audience can't predict how you'll show up or what you stand for, they will hesitate to invest attention. This doesn't mean you must remain static. On the contrary, audiences respect growth. But they need to feel that your evolution is grounded in values rather than vanity. That your changes are driven by insight, not insecurity. When they sense that, they follow not just what you say, but why you say it, and that is when trust starts to form.

Beyond clarity, trust also requires congruence. It is not enough to say the right things. Your behavior must reflect your message. If you write about generosity but react with pettiness to criticism, the audience will notice. If you preach strategy but post impulsively, they'll register the contradiction. These minor dissonances accumulate quickly. People are more attuned than ever to inconsistencies, and they have little tolerance for what feels performative. On the other hand, when your words and actions align, and your online posture reflects your offline perspective, people begin to lean in. They begin to believe you.

Congruence doesn't mean perfection. Flaws, when owned, often increase trust. What erodes trust isn't error, it's evasion. When you pretend to be above reproach, when you delete dissent or double down in defensiveness, you communicate fragility. But when you acknowledge missteps with humility, when you clarify rather than obfuscate, you create space for the audience to trust not your infallibility, but your honesty. And honesty, in the context of digital presence, is the rarest and most potent form of leverage there is.

The compounding effect of trust cannot be overstated. When your audience trusts you, they become your distribution engine. Not because you asked, but because they want others to hear what you have to say. They forward your work. They quote you in presentations. They reference your frameworks, not as evangelists, but as partners in perspective. You become part of their internal narrative, not just someone they follow, but someone whose thinking has helped them think better.

And when trust reaches this level, it unlocks not just content, but relevance. You don't just have an audience; you have a role. People turn to you at inflection points. They seek your take on complex issues. They trust you to interpret new developments. You become not just a source of information, but a lens through which they view the world. That is the highest form of digital presence, not being seen, but being *used* in the best sense of the word. You become a tool for their clarity, a resource for their decisions, a voice they carry into their leadership and communication.

But none of this happens by accident. Trust is not a byproduct of growth. It is a precondition of influence. And building it requires both philosophical commitment and tactical execution. It demands that you see every piece of content not as a chance to perform, but as an opportunity to reinforce belief. Not just belief in your ideas, but belief in your intent, your orientation, your willingness to serve rather than exploit.

To build trust at scale, you must start by being trustworthy at the granular level. This means paying attention not only to what you publish but also to how you respond. In the early days of audience growth, it's tempting to treat feedback, questions, or disagreement as distractions. But these moments are not interruptions; they are invitations. Every thoughtful comment is a small test of your posture, and how you show up in those exchanges does more to build or break trust than any piece of content you might schedule in advance.

Responding with care signals that you are not merely broadcasting but listening. That you are willing to meet people where they are, not just where you wish they'd be. It communicates respect, and respect is one of the fastest accelerants of trust. When people feel seen, not as metrics, but as minds, they begin to open up. They begin to share more freely. They return not just to consume but to participate.

This is how communities form, not around a product, not around a brand, but around a voice that feels dependable. That voice becomes a stabilizing force in a chaotic feed. Not because it always agrees with the audience, but because it always respects them. This kind of consistency earns the right to challenge, to provoke, even to disagree, because the foundation of trust has already been established.

What many creators and thought leaders fail to understand is that trust is not static. It is dynamic, constantly influenced by context. You may have built a strong presence over months or years, but one moment of perceived inauthenticity can shift the entire perception of your work. This isn't because audiences are unforgiving; it's because trust exists in tension with power. As your influence grows, so does the weight of your words. The more people look to you, the more they expect of you. And while that may feel unfair, it is the cost of visibility with meaning.

This is why high-trust creators often adopt a slower, more intentional cadence. They know that each post, each response, each public stance carries compound consequences. They don't fear the consequences, but they do respect them. That respect shows up in their tone, in their research, in their unwillingness to publish half-formed opinions for the sake of participating in a trend. They wait. They think. They speak with care. And the result is a kind of resonance that more reactive creators can't mimic.

The irony is that trust-based presence is often quieter than its high-engagement counterparts. It does not always dominate the trending lists. It does not generate controversy for attention. But it lasts. And that longevity becomes leverage. While others burn out from trying to maintain relevance, trusted creators grow in influence by deepening it. Their reach may not spike, but their impact deepens. Their words linger. Their ideas circulate. Their silence is even felt, not as absence, but as anticipation.

That anticipation is a powerful form of leverage. It flips the dynamic of content creation. Instead of chasing the audience, the audience begins to wait for you. They come to rely on your cadence, your lens, your way of framing what matters. And because they trust that what you share will be worth their time, they give you something rare in the digital age: patience.

Patience, once earned, gives you room to grow. It permits you to take risks, to change directions, to experiment with new formats or topics. Your audience does not punish you for evolving; they support it because they believe in the person behind the evolution. They are not here just for one kind of content. They are here for *you*. That distinction is the essence of creator leverage. It's what separates transient popularity from enduring presence.

Leverage built on trust also changes your relationship to monetization. In low-trust environments, every offer must be justified, every promotion questioned. Audiences become suspicious, interpreting every shift as a potential betrayal. But in high-trust relationships, the offer is often welcomed. Not because people are unthinkingly loyal, but because they believe that what you're offering comes from the same place as your content: usefulness, clarity, and intent. They trust that you're not selling them out; you're inviting them further in.

This is why creators who focus exclusively on audience growth without cultivating trust often find themselves stuck. They build large followings that don't convert, that don't engage deeply, that vanish as quickly as they appeared. What's missing is not reach; it's the relationship. And relationships, unlike impressions, do not scale without intention. They must be fostered, protected, and honored.

Honoring the audience is not about flattery. It's about accuracy. It's about knowing who they are, what they struggle with, and what they hope for. It's about speaking to them in ways that reflect their intelligence, their complexity, and their curiosity. Too many creators dumb down their message in pursuit of reach, forgetting that attention gained by underestimating the audience rarely turns into trust. In contrast, speaking to the highest in your audience, without alienating the rest, signals that you believe they're capable of more. And belief is a powerful trust signal.

The creators who master this balance build not just platforms, but ecosystems. They become more than content producers. They become guides, facilitators, even stewards of a particular worldview. Their work doesn't just inform, it shapes. Their presence doesn't just attract, it orients. And their audience doesn't just follow, they engage, build, and extend the vision in ways the creator alone could never achieve.

This is trust as leverage. Not just to gain influence, but to enable transformation.

Trust, once established and nurtured, begins to replace the scaffolding that others rely on. Where many creators depend on tricks of visibility, timing their posts to align with peak engagement windows, reverse-engineering content formats based on trending sounds or headline formulas, you find that trust shifts the burden of performance away from the surface and into the substance. What once required effortful orchestration now flows with a kind of earned simplicity. Your presence holds because people expect it to. Not because they've been nudged, reminded, or interrupted, but because they've internalized its value.

This transition from attention-seeking to trust-based resonance redefines your operational reality. You no longer create solely for conversion. You have to maintain coherence. You make to sharpen your thinking, to articulate the unsaid, to offer frameworks that illuminate. Revenue, audience growth, and brand authority may still matter, but they're byproducts of a deeper relationship. You've become a part of someone's intellectual and emotional infrastructure. You help them make sense of things, not just the world, but themselves within it.

That kind of trust does not tether you to a specific platform or format. It liberates you. A creator who has earned trust can move mediums without losing relevance. Their audience follows, not because of habit, but because of attachment. That attachment isn't emotional in a shallow, parasocial sense. It's architectural. People have built something inside themselves using your words, your models, your voice. When you shift, they want to preserve the connection, not out of nostalgia, but because it still serves them.

This is why creators with deep trust often succeed across mediums, from writing to speaking to teaching to product creation. The format changes, but the promise remains the same. That promise is not about access or entertainment. It's about clarity. Your presence becomes a filter. When the world becomes noisy, they turn to you for a signal. When things feel complex, they trust you to simplify without dumbing down. When they feel uncertain, they return to your work not for answers necessarily, but for orientation.

Orientation is one of the highest forms of value you can offer. In an age where most people are overwhelmed not by scarcity of information but by abundance of interpretation, the trusted creator becomes a compass, not by positioning themselves as an oracle, but by embodying a kind of discernment that feels rare and grounded. You don't need to be right all the time. You need to be transparent about how you think, how you weigh, and how you revise. That kind of transparency breeds an even deeper form of trust: epistemic trust—the trust not just in what you know, but in how you know it.

That level of trust unlocks a very different kind of influence, an influence that works quietly, often invisibly, but with far greater durability. It's the kind of influence that doesn't require the platform to validate it. It's felt in rooms you're not in, in decisions you didn't directly touch, in strategies that bear your fingerprints even if your name isn't attached. Your ideas begin to have second-order effects. They shape those who shape others.

And that is the essence of proper creative leverage. You stop playing the visibility game on its terms. You begin to set your own. The work becomes more personal, yet less self-centered. More reflective, yet more expansive. You become the kind of creator who is not only followed but referenced. Not only consumed but consulted, and not only heard but remembered.

But even as this level of trust deepens your influence, it requires maintenance, not in the performative sense of maintaining an image, but in the ethical sense of maintaining alignment. The more people believe in you, the more damaging your missteps become, not because people expect perfection, but because they've come to rely on your consistency. You carry a different kind of responsibility. Not the burden of being faultless, but the discipline of being aware.

This is where many creators falter, not from evil intent, but from neglect. They forget that the trust they've built is not a static asset. It's a living relationship. It needs presence. It needs a signal. It needs reflection. And when it's neglected, the loss is slow but definitive. People drift. Not out of anger, but out of disappointment. The voice that once centered them now feels distant. The clarity that once cut through the noise is muffled. They move on, not with drama, but with quiet resolution.

To sustain trust, then, is to commit to constant re-attunement. You must continue to listen, not just to feedback, but to changes in the cultural and intellectual environment. You must remain open to refinement, to tension, to challenge. And you must keep the channel between who you are and how you show up as clear as possible. When that alignment holds, your presence becomes not just consistent, it becomes generative.

A generative presence creates more than content. It creates context. It allows others to see themselves more clearly, to engage more deeply, to contribute more meaningfully. You become a source not just of ideas, but of energy. And in the economy of digital presence, that energy compounds far more powerfully than attention.

As this chapter draws to a close, the arc should be clear. Trust is not a feature of your brand. It is the foundation. It is what makes all the other levers work. Without it, your content is decoration. With it, your presence becomes infrastructure. You can influence without manipulating. You can scale without splintering. You can lead without posturing. Because the people who follow you do so not for a hit of dopamine, but for a return to depth.

In the age of the feed, that is revolutionary.

Chapter Eight: Depth Over Reach

In every corner of digital culture, from newsletters to LinkedIn posts to the chaotic churn of TikTok, the dominant metric is always reach. How far did it travel? How many eyes saw it? How many impressions, clicks, opens, or views? Reach is the drug that fuels the attention economy, and most of us are hooked before we even know we're using it. The platforms reward it, advertisers demand it, and creators chase it, often without questioning its value or cost. But beneath that pursuit lies a quieter truth: reach is usually a mirage. It looks like influence, but it isn't. It seems like traction, but it doesn't always translate. What moves fast doesn't always go deep, and what goes deep rarely moves fast.

Depth, by contrast, is less glamorous. It rarely trends. It doesn't make headlines. But it lasts. Depth is what makes someone not just pause, but stay. It's what compels someone to revisit a post days later, to share it in private circles, to cite it in a meeting, to alter their behavior in subtle and persistent ways. You don't need a million impressions to have an impact. You need to change the minds of a few hundred people. Because those minds talk, they act. They multiply. Depth scales sideways, not upward.

The problem is that most creators are conditioned to prioritize virality over value. The first question they ask when drafting a post isn't, "What is the most useful thing I can say?" It's "What will travel?" But this framework backfires. Content designed purely for reach is often hollow. It gets the click, maybe even the comment, but it rarely changes anyone. It flatters rather than challenges. It entertains rather than clarifies. And over time, it builds an audience that expects novelty, not substance. The creator becomes trapped in a cycle of diminishing returns, each post more extreme, more reactive, more diluted than the last, to keep pace with expectations they didn't mean to set. Meanwhile, creators who commit to depth often grow more slowly. Their posts don't always pop. Their ideas take time to digest. Their reach may look modest on the surface. But their audience is listening, thinking, integrating. And that kind of attention, real attention, is rarer and more potent than any follower count. It creates a foundation on which trust, authority, and transformation can be built. It is the kind of attention that returns even in your absence. It remembers. It evolves. It spreads not through metrics, but through meaning.

Creating depth means asking a different set of questions. Not "How can I go viral?" but "What can I say that matters even if only fifty people hear it?" Not "What's trending right now?" but "What's timeless within this topic?" Not "How do I capture attention?" but "How do I reward it?" These questions don't make you famous overnight, but they position you as someone whose work can't be ignored once discovered.

This shift in orientation is not easy. Platforms are designed to optimize for visibility, not value. Their incentives are temporal, not intellectual. They reward frequency, not reflection. So creating depth requires a kind of resistance. A willingness to post less often, but more intentionally. A commitment to producing work that stands on its own, regardless of algorithmic favor. And perhaps most of all, a long view, an understanding that lasting influence accrues through thoughtful iteration, not explosive traction.

Depth is also an antidote to the burnout that plagues high-reach creators. When you build an audience by saying what everyone else is saying, only louder or faster, you lock yourself into a performance loop. You have to keep escalating to maintain interest. But when you build through depth, through clarity, originality, and resonance, you give yourself room to breathe. Your audience doesn't demand constant novelty. They return because they know you're crafting ideas worth sitting with. They expect quality, not volume. And that expectation grants you the space to think deeply, to research carefully, to write with intent.

This kind of audience is smaller, yes, but it is far more stable. It doesn't evaporate when the algorithm changes. It doesn't disappear during your off weeks. It doesn't penalize you for being human. Instead, it evolves alongside you. It grows not through spectacle, but through alignment. When you change, your audience adapts. When you challenge them, they respond. And when you disappear for a while, they're still there when you return, not because they need your content to fill a gap in their feed, but because your presence has filled a gap in their thinking.

Reaching this point requires more than just good content. It requires coherence across time. Your ideas must be traceable. Your body of work must reflect an arc. That doesn't mean you have to say the same thing forever; it means your evolution must make sense. Your early work should connect to your current thinking, even if only by contrast. Your voice should sharpen, not fracture. Your perspective should deepen, not scatter. And most importantly, your intention must be legible.

Legibility of intention is the bedrock of depth. When your audience understands not just what you say, but why you say it, they begin to follow you not for any single idea, but for your entire orientation. They trust your lens. They learn from your shifts. They begin to use you as a proxy for navigating their uncertainties. And that trust, once formed, allows you to go deeper still. You no longer have to justify every deviation or contextualize every choice. They know you. They know your rhythm. They stay with you not out of habit, but out of choice.

Depth is not simply a matter of writing longer pieces or including more data points. It's about entering the mind of your audience and staying there. A deep idea lingers not because it dazzles, but because it reshapes. It changes the contours of a problem, alters the language someone uses to describe their world, or reframes a pattern they hadn't noticed. When someone says, "I've never thought about it that way before," that is the sound of depth at work.

This shift is not achieved through cleverness. Cleverness performs. Depth transforms. Cleverness wants to be noticed. Depth is intended to be used. Cleverness demands applause. Depth creates silence, the kind that follows insight. And insight is a strange currency in the attention economy. It doesn't always register immediately. It often skips the metrics entirely, taking root in quieter ways, in how someone handles a conversation, in a decision they revise later, in a pattern they begin to question.

For creators seeking long-term relevance, this is the only game worth playing. The game of being remembered, not simply noticed. Of building frameworks, not just delivering quotes. Of becoming someone whose work shows up in meetings, in emails, in strategy decks, often without attribution, and sometimes without your name even attached, because the idea has already outgrown you. That is when you know your work has depth, when it begins to live a second life without your help.

But creating this kind of work requires discipline not just in writing, but in listening. Depth comes from sustained observation of your audience, yes, but also of your thinking. You have to watch what you're drawn to, what you avoid, what you say out of habit, and what you've stopped examining. You have to develop an inner radar for borrowed opinions, for recycled insights, for elegant but empty phrasing. And you have to resist the temptation to say what is merely adjacent to the truth to meet the moment.

This is why deep creators often have slower publishing cadences. It's not because they're perfectionists, though some are. It's because they know the cost of releasing something half-baked. Not the reputational cost, most people won't even notice, but the cognitive one. Every shallow post reinforces a pattern in the creator's mind. It makes it harder to go deep next time. It trains the creator to be reactive, optimizing for reach over relevance. And over time, that optimization becomes internalized. They lose access to their original voice, buried beneath layers of performance.

Going deep means opting out of that cycle. It means writing even when you don't have something viral to say. It means publishing pieces that feel quiet, but true. It means returning to ideas not because they're hot, but because they're unfinished. And it means understanding that the real impact of your work may not appear for weeks, months, or even years. Some of the most powerful writing you'll do will not gain traction immediately. It will sit, dormant, until the world catches up, or until one person stumbles across it at precisely the right moment. That one person might change everything.

Depth is also an act of self-trust. You must believe that what you're creating matters, even when the data doesn't validate it. This is particularly hard in a world where feedback is constant, public, and often brutal. When a shallow post performs well and a thoughtful essay lands with silence, the temptation is to shift your strategy. But depth requires patience. It requires faith in the compounding nature of quality. It asks you to build the kind of archive that, while perhaps under-appreciated now, becomes a well others return to when the noise has passed.

The irony is that, over time, deep work often earns more reach than the shallow kind. Not through immediate virality, but through sustained referral. Through the slow, steady force of recommendation. People send their work to others because it helps clarify things. Because it resonates. Because it holds. And while that kind of reach may not show up on a chart, it is far more valuable. It creates audience members who stay, not because you keep chasing them, but because they've anchored part of their perspective to your work.

You become not a source of updates, but a source of orientation.

This role, of guide, rather than entertainer, is not for everyone. It carries responsibility. It requires boundaries, not to keep people out, but to keep your thinking intact. It demands time away from the feed, away from the metrics, away from the performance of presence. It requires solitude. Not isolation, but the kind of solitude that lets thoughts mature without interruption. That enables a paragraph to breathe before it's posted. That allows an idea to take shape in silence.

This is the internal rhythm of depth. It doesn't pulse with the tempo of trends. It grows quietly, underground. And then, without warning, it erupts. Not in the form of a viral post, but in the shape of an ecosystem. An audience that trusts you. A body of work that holds together. A reputation that no algorithm can erase. A presence that survives the platforms it was born on.

In this sense, depth is not just a strategy. It is a philosophy. A refusal to be manipulated by the urgent. A commitment to serving the enduring. And while it may take longer and feel lonelier, it is the only way to build something that matters, not just for this moment, but for the many that follow.

The pursuit of depth, when fully embraced, forces a re-evaluation of success itself. No longer do follower counts or algorithmic boosts hold the same appeal. Instead, the creator begins to measure success by the quality of conversations their work initiates, by the caliber of individuals who choose to engage, and by the way their content travels not as entertainment, but as utility. When you begin to track your influence by the sophistication of the audience it gathers, rather than its size, the creative process transforms. It becomes more grounded, more demanding, and infinitely more rewarding.

To create depth is to invest in future relevance. You are not trying to dominate the conversation today. You are planting intellectual seeds in your audience's minds, trusting that they will germinate over time. Some ideas will lie dormant until the conditions are right, until a new context arises, or until someone revisits your work with a different set of experiences. And when they do, your content doesn't feel dated. It feels prescient. Because it was never about the moment, it was about the undercurrent.

That undercurrent is what real thought leadership consists of, not the regurgitation of today's headlines, but the articulation of tomorrow's frameworks. It's about giving people a way to think, not just a thing to think about. When you do this well, you become a kind of cognitive companion. People return to your work not to be entertained, but to be reoriented. To remember what matters. To strip away the noise and rediscover the signal.

This is why depth repels superficiality. Once you start creating for meaning, you lose your tolerance for cheap attention. You stop chasing the dopamine hit of likes and begin to chase clarity instead. The game shifts from volume to precision. From reach to resonance. And with that shift comes a surprising side effect: peace. You no longer feel beholden to trends. You stop measuring yourself against the metrics of strangers. You begin to inhabit your lane fully, without apology or artifice.

But make no mistake, this is not a passive stance. It is not a withdrawal. It is a commitment to playing a different game altogether. One where influence is built slowly, ethically, through relationships and rigor. One where each piece of content is a brick in something larger, a thesis, a worldview, a movement. You are not trying to dominate the moment. You are building a cathedral of ideas. And cathedrals, by nature, are not built in haste.

This long-term orientation requires resilience. There will be moments when you question the path, when others with shallower strategies seem to surge ahead, when your posts are met with silence. When your best work seems invisible, but in those moments, you return to your values. You remember why you chose this path in the first place, not to impress, but to endure. Not to trend, but to teach. Not to entertain, but to equip.

And slowly, the results begin to appear, not in the virality of a post, but in the intimacy of an email reply that says, "This changed how I think." Not in the speed of your growth, but in the sturdiness of it. Not in the explosion of metrics, but in the quiet, steady pressure of being cited, referenced, and returned to. You realize that you are no longer just publishing content. You are shaping thought. You are participating in the architecture of how people make meaning in the world.

Depth is not a strategy for everyone. It requires intellectual humility, emotional endurance, and a deep-seated belief that better is more important than bigger. It is, in many ways, a contrarian stance. In a world that rewards surface, it is a commitment to substance. In a system that values reaction, it is a commitment to reflection. In a culture that obsesses over virality, it is a commitment to longevity.

But for those willing to make that commitment, the rewards are unlike anything the pursuit of reach can offer. You don't just gain followers, you gain advocates. You don't just gain visibility, you gain reverence. You don't just gain momentum, you gain meaning. And perhaps most importantly, you gain the ability to keep going, not because you're chasing attention, but because you've created something that continues to matter, regardless of whether anyone is watching in the moment.

That is the ultimate power of depth. It allows you to disappear without vanishing. To step back without falling behind. To slow down without losing relevance. Because depth, once established, doesn't evaporate. It lingers. It echoes. It anchors. It gives you a home inside the minds of others, a space you earned not by being loud, but by being clear, not by being seen, but by being remembered.

And in a world that forgets almost everything it consumes, to be remembered is to have won.

Chapter Nine: Algorithms Aren't Neutral

For years, the dominant narrative around social media platforms and content discovery engines has been that they operate according to some cold, impartial logic. The term "algorithm" itself carries a sort of mystique, a promise that behind the scenes, math is making the decisions. Neutral. Unbiased. Fair. This framing is not just misleading; it's actively dangerous. Algorithms are not neutral. They are not objective arbiters of relevance or truth. They are designed systems with specific incentives, specific values, most of which are invisible to the user but profoundly influential in shaping what gets seen, what gains traction, and ultimately, what becomes culturally dominant.

To believe otherwise is to misunderstand the terrain you're operating on. You are not navigating a public square. You're operating inside someone else's casino, one where the rules change without notice, where the house always wins, and where your attention is the currency being gambled. The algorithm is not curated for quality. It is optimizing for outcomes that serve the platform's interests. These interests are not secret. They revolve around engagement, retention, ad revenue, and growth. And every decision the algorithm makes, every tweak it undergoes, is in service of those outcomes, not yours.

Creators often enter the digital landscape assuming that good content will rise. That value will naturally float to the top. But this assumption ignores the fundamental design of algorithmic systems. They are not designed to surface the best content. They are designed to surface the content that keeps people scrolling.

That's not the same thing. Those two outcomes often diverge. Content that is nuanced, slow-burning, or challenging tends to perform poorly in systems built for rapid-fire interaction. At the same time, content that is polarizing, emotionally manipulative, or visually sensational performs exceedingly well.

This dynamic has consequences. It creates a feedback loop in which creators feel pressured to produce what the algorithm rewards, even if it contradicts their values or diminishes the quality of their work. Over time, the creator begins to internalize those incentives. They don't just adjust their tactics; they reshape their voice. They start second-guessing their instincts, diluting their ideas, compressing their arguments to fit into formats that favor speed over depth, spectacle over substance.

And it's not just individuals who suffer. Entire industries, entire conversations, begin to shift in response to algorithmic gravity. Health professionals simplify their messaging to fit TikTok formats. Journalists frame headlines for maximum click potential. Academics reduce complex research into digestible soundbites. In doing so, nuance is lost. Context is erased. The medium begins to dictate the message, and the platform's values start to overwrite our own.

None of this is accidental. It's the product of deliberate design. Algorithms are engineered by teams of people, working within companies that are accountable not to truth or social good, but to shareholders. That's not a conspiracy; it's a structural reality. These systems are built with a primary mandate: to maximize user engagement. Every other priority, accuracy, wellbeing, representation, and intellectual depth, is secondary at best, if considered at all. So when we treat the algorithm as a neutral force, we are abdicating our responsibility as both creators and consumers.

Creators, in particular, must approach algorithms not with reverence, but with realism. Some impartial judge of merit is not evaluating you. You are being filtered through a machine trained to predict what will keep people on the platform longer. Sometimes that aligns with thoughtful content. Often it doesn't. And if you build your entire strategy around pleasing that machine, you may achieve reach, but you will struggle to maintain integrity.

So what does it mean to create in an environment where algorithms are not neutral? It means designing your strategy with a complete understanding of the constraints. It means recognizing when to play within the system and when to opt out. It means creating parallel channels, newsletters, podcasts, and private communities where your content can thrive beyond the whims of algorithmic favor. It means prioritizing work that fosters trust and resonance over time, rather than chasing the fleeting success of platform optimization.

But perhaps most importantly, it means interrogating your reflexes when you find yourself altering a headline to make it "pop," and asking why. When you hesitate to share something meaningful because it's not "on trend," examine what values you're prioritizing. When you rewrite a paragraph to make it more shareable, consider whether you've sacrificed clarity for clickability. These are not easy questions, but they are necessary ones. Because every time you adjust your work to fit an algorithm's preferences, you are reshaping not just your message, but your mind.

It's easy to blame the platforms. And they deserve their share of critique. But the more urgent responsibility lies with us. We must become conscious participants in these systems, rather than passive subjects. We must develop internal standards for quality that are not dependent on external validation. We must learn to recognize when our creative instincts are being hijacked by incentives we never agreed to. And we must teach our audiences to expect more, to value clarity over controversy, coherence over virality.

Because if we don't, we become complicit in the erosion of attention, the degradation of discourse, and the slow, silent substitution of entertainment for enlightenment.

When creators begin to resist algorithmic coercion, the results are not always immediate. There is, at first, a friction that can feel punishing. A thoughtful post might be met with silence. A well-reasoned argument might get buried beneath less nuanced clickbait. And that dissonance can be demoralizing. It creates the illusion that substance doesn't matter, that speed and spectacle have triumphed for good. But that illusion only holds if you assume that the algorithm is the sole terrain of value. It isn't. It's just the most visible terrain, the loudest, not the deepest.

There is a different layer of interaction unfolding beneath the metrics. It's harder to measure, harder to prove, but it's where actual impact lives. These are the private shares, the forwarded emails, the bookmarked essays, the conversations sparked in rooms you'll never enter. These are the consequences that don't go viral, but that shift someone's direction. And often, these shifts are born from content that the algorithm buried, not because it was weak, but because it was slow. Because it required attention, and the machine is trained to prize compulsion instead. This dissonance becomes your training ground. It forces you to develop a new kind of muscle, not the one that performs for attention, but the one that persists without it. You learn to create with integrity even when applause is withheld. You learn to trust the long game. You begin to see that visibility and value are not synonyms. That resonance does not always correlate with reach. And that the quality of your audience, their intelligence, their intent, their capacity for influence, matters far more than their quantity.

Creators who survive this phase develop something rare: independence from platform psychology. They stop checking metrics obsessively. They stop chasing likes as a proxy for truth. They stop overreacting to algorithmic changes. Instead, they focus on creating a body of work that reflects a consistent point of view, a clear voice, a discernible arc. They stop trying to win a game they don't control and start building something they do.

That's not to say you ignore the algorithm altogether. You learn to be aware without being obedient. You understand its logic without being governed by it. You identify when it can serve your goals, and when it can't. And when it can't, you stop bending. You let the piece be what it needs to be, not what the system wants it to become. This is creative sovereignty: the ability to publish what is true, regardless of how it performs.

It is also a competitive advantage. Because most creators never reach this stage. They stay caught in the loop, creating for the algorithm, adjusting their voice, building a persona that maximizes engagement but minimizes connection. And eventually, that loop burns them out. They run out of content. They lose their audience. Or worse, they lose themselves. Their voice becomes an echo chamber of what worked before, no longer reflective, no longer adaptive—just more noise.

The creators who resist that fate do something different. They create in layers. There's the surface layer, algorithmically legible content, that meets the platform's minimum requirements for visibility. But beneath that is a deeper layer: a body of thought that matures over time. That layer is what your most discerning audience members will come back for. It's what gives your work staying power. It's what makes your ideas worth quoting, referencing, and building upon. It's what makes your silence feel deliberate, not absent.

This layered approach is not a trick. It's not a way to hack the algorithm. It's a strategy for surviving it and for building something that can grow in hostile soil. To ensure that your online presence is defined by substance, not volatility. And when you do it well, the algorithm begins to shift around you. Not because you've gamed it, but because you've created something the system wasn't designed to contain, work that travels not by design, but by demand.

Demand is a very different force from distribution. Distribution is what the platform grants you when you play by its rules. Demand is what your audience creates when your work is irreplaceable. Distribution can be revoked overnight. Demand endures. It is what keeps people searching for your name even when the feed forgets you. What keeps your ideas circulating even when the platform doesn't boost them? What builds a moat around your work that no algorithmic shift can erode?

To cultivate this kind of demand, you must build with intentional constraints. You must choose formats that reward depth. You must craft ideas that invite participation rather than passive consumption. You must create a brand that does not rest on frequency, but on fidelity. And you must do all this while resisting the internalized belief that visibility equals value. That belief is poison. It shrinks your ambition to what is currently legible. It turns you into a mimic of what works, rather than an author of what matters.

Instead, you develop a different ambition, not to dominate the feed, but to change the frame. Not to accumulate views, but to distribute vision. Not to be everywhere, but to be essential wherever you are.

This is not just a shift in strategy. It's a shift in self-concept. You stop thinking of yourself as a content producer and start thinking of yourself as a cultural node. As a transmitter of ideas that reorganize people's perception. And that reorganization, of thought, of language, of attention, is the most powerful form of influence you can wield.

Algorithms can distribute content. But only creators can distribute thought.

To build thought that travels, that endures, that resists the compression of algorithmic logic, you must step outside the temporal demands of the platform. You must create as if you're not being watched. You must return to the original intention that brought you here, to communicate something real, to articulate what others feel but cannot say, to name the patterns behind the noise. The moment you detach your creative process from the algorithm's metrics, something strange happens: your clarity returns. You begin to write for people again, not for the machine. And people, unlike algorithms, remember you for how you made them think.

This clarity doesn't make you naive about the system. You still understand its mechanics. You still know how it influences distribution. But now you see it for what it is: a tool, not a truth. And like any tool, it can be used, ignored, or replaced. You stop chasing virality because you understand it offers no guarantee of longevity. You stop obsessing over frequency because you know that one piece of deeply resonant work can outweigh months of filler. And you stop asking the algorithm to validate your worth because you know that real validation comes from connection, not clicks.

The creators who succeed in this new orientation tend to have something in common: they build infrastructure around their ideas. They don't rely on one platform. They don't pour all their energy into a single feed. Instead, they create layers, newsletters, podcasts, private groups, and long-form essays that serve as alternative distribution channels. Channels that grow slower, yes, but also stronger. Channels that offer insulation from algorithmic volatility. Channels that allow for a different kind of intimacy, one where the creator and the audience meet without intermediaries.

This infrastructure is not just a hedge against platform risk. It is an act of creative independence. When you control your distribution, you control your pacing, your tone, and your priorities. You are no longer sprinting to keep up with the feed. You are walking at your cadence, inviting others to walk with you. And those who walk with you aren't there for spectacle, they're there for substance. They're not following you out of habit, but because your work has become a part of how they think.

This kind of relationship is fragile, but powerful. It cannot be bought. AI cannot manufacture it. Engagement tricks cannot fake it. It must be earned. And it is earned not by playing the algorithm's game better than everyone else, but by refusing to let that game define your creative choices.

This refusal is radical because everything around you will tempt you to compromise. The trending topics. The analytics dashboards. The other creators whose shallow work seems to outperform yours. The slow feedback loops make you question whether your approach is even working. And sometimes, yes, you will be tempted. You'll draft a tweet that feels slick but hollow. You'll rewrite a headline to juice the clicks. You'll wonder if maybe, just maybe, you should play along for a while.

But then you'll remember: every compromise you make in the direction of visibility is a tax on clarity. A trust tax. A tax on the kind of influence that compounds slowly, but definitively. And once you've tasted that kind of influence, you'll realize that no viral post, no algorithmic boost, no fleeting trend is worth losing it. Because the impact you're here to create doesn't live on the surface. It lives in the slow accumulation of trust, insight, and presence.

This kind of impact doesn't just shape audiences. It shapes industries. It shifts conversations. It builds reputations that outlast platforms. And that is the point. You are not building a career inside someone else's feed. You are creating a body of work that can move across formats, across years, across cultures. You are not a content creator. You are a context creator. A voice that organizes chaos into coherence. A presence that outlasts the infrastructure that first carried it.

The algorithm will constantly evolve. Its signals will change. Its rules will mutate. What worked last year will stop working tomorrow. And if your identity is tethered to its logic, you will be dragged along with it, constantly adapting, pivoting, never arriving. But if your work is rooted in something more profound, clarity, coherence, and intention, you become untouchable. You are no longer subject to the feed. You are building something that can't be scrolled past.

That's the real rebellion in the age of algorithmic dominance, not louder content, but clearer thought. Not faster output, but more profound insight. Not more followers, but a sharper lens. Because when the system trains us to crave exposure, the most subversive thing we can do is prioritize understanding.

So write the post that doesn't trend. Publish the essay that's too long for the feed. Make the video that doesn't open with a hook. Say the thing that makes people pause, not just react. And do it knowing that it might not go viral. That it might not be rewarded. That it might disappear into the scroll. But also knowing that someone, somewhere, needed it. And that, in giving it to them without pandering, you've done something rare.

You've created outside the machine.

And in doing so, you've begun to break the algorithm.

Chapter Ten: Legacy Work in a Disposable Culture

We live in an age where digital ephemera defines the pace of our lives. A post might make waves for a day, a video might surge for a weekend, a headline might dominate discourse for seventy-two hours, and then, nothing. The feed moves on, always hungry, constantly devouring, never satisfied. In this climate, most content is built to expire. It is made for the moment, not the decade. It is designed to satisfy, not to endure. And creators, often unconsciously, absorb that ethos. They begin to create with the assumption that their work will be forgotten. That longevity is naïve. That speed is strategy. That repetition is relevant. This is the logic of disposability. And it is killing the impulse to build something that lasts.

Legacy work is the opposite of this instinct. It is not produced for attention, but for consequence. Its virality does not judge it, but by its staying power. It is the kind of work that does not move quickly through the world, but settles into it. It gains weight over time. It accrues meaning in retrospect. It becomes, years later, the thing people point to and say, "That's where it changed." It is not flashy. It is not always immediately understood. But it lingers. And that lingering is the most powerful signal of all.

Creating legacy work in a culture of disposability requires an extraordinary kind of defiance. You are choosing to develop slowly in a world that rewards the fast. You are choosing to craft when others churn. You are choosing to go deep when the system rewards staying light. And perhaps most counterintuitively, you are choosing to be misunderstood in the short term for the possibility of being indispensable in the long term. That kind of wager is not for the faint of heart.

It starts with a different orientation to time. Most creators today operate in a cycle dictated by platform metrics, daily posting, weekly emails, and quarterly campaigns. The pressure to remain visible is constant. The assumption is that absence equals irrelevance. But legacy work resists that tempo. It requires periods of incubation, of silence, of wandering. It asks you to prioritize the arc of your thinking over the velocity of your output. It forces you to consider not just what will resonate today, but what might still hold meaning in five years, or ten. That question, What will still matter?, becomes the compass.

And what tends to matter, long after the flash has faded, is rarely the clever turn of phrase or the perfectly optimized thumbnail. It is the clarity of thought—the emotional honesty. The risk is embedded in the idea. It is the work that reflects a mind willing to stand alone. Not to provoke, but to withstand dismissal. Not to antagonize, but to endure solitude. Legacy work almost always begins in obscurity. Not because it's weak, but because it's early. Because it hasn't found its time yet. Because it demands more of the audience than the culture is ready to give.

This is where many creators falter. They take the silence as a sign to pivot. They dilute the message. They adapt to what's working now, never realizing that what's working now is the very thing that will be forgotten next. And so they miss the opportunity to build something foundational, something that could have become reference material, had they stayed the course.

Legacy work also requires a different relationship to influence. Most creators today seek influence as a form of social proof: the bigger the audience, the more credible the voice. But legacy creators understand influence differently. For them, influence is not about breadth, but about depth. It is not about how many people know your name, but how deeply your work is embedded in the decisions they make, the frameworks they adopt, and the questions they begin to ask. Actual influence doesn't announce itself. It infiltrates. It reorganizes. It shows up in places where your name is never mentioned, but your ideas are present, nonetheless.

This kind of influence cannot be gamed. It cannot be reverse-engineered through brand partnerships or distribution hacks. It is the result of consistency, clarity, and an unshakable fidelity to the work itself. It is earned, slowly, through accumulation. Through showing up when it doesn't pay off. Through writing, when no one is reading. Through refining an idea across years of iteration, until it becomes undeniable. Until it moves from being an interesting take to being the default lens.

And once that happens, something shifts. The culture begins to reorganize around the work. People who once dismissed it begin to cite it. Institutions that once ignored it are now adopting it. Competitors start to mimic it. And suddenly, what was once fringe becomes foundational. What was once eccentric becomes canon. This is the strange alchemy of legacy. It moves from the margins to the center, but only when the creator has the patience to remain unmoved by the center's initial indifference.

The center, after all, rarely recognizes what it needs in real time. It consumes, reacts, and rewards what is easiest to metabolize. It prefers content that affirms its existing beliefs, that fits within its existing categories. Legacy work doesn't do that. It disrupts categories. It calls into question the very assumptions the center is built on. And because of that, it is often mischaracterized or ignored until it becomes too valuable to overlook. This delay is not a failure of the work; it is a feature of it. Legacy is what emerges when an idea, initially resisted, proves indispensable over time.

But creating with that kind of delayed gratification in mind demands a different type of inner ecology. You must become less reactive to praise and more resilient to neglect. You must develop a creative immune system that filters out the noise of premature judgment because early metrics are rarely predictive. Some of the most influential ideas in history began as private journals, self-published pamphlets, and overlooked lectures. Their initial impact was minimal, but their eventual reach was seismic. That kind of reach is not built on trend alignment. It is built on structural clarity, the type of clarity that survives changing contexts.

This is why legacy creators often appear out of sync with the dominant aesthetic of their time. They are not ignoring the culture; they're moving beneath it. They're engaging at a different depth, planting seeds in soil that hasn't yet shown signs of life. And when the culture finally catches up, their work is already fully formed. It doesn't need to be adjusted. It doesn't scramble to be relevant. It simply rises to meet the moment it was made for.

That readiness requires rigor. You cannot create legacy work casually. You can't post your way into enduring significance.

You have to shape, refine, and rework your ideas. You have to interrogate your assumptions. You have to read deeply, think slowly, and resist the compulsion to publish before the idea is ripe. In a disposable culture, where the half-baked is rewarded and the polished is often overlooked, this discipline can feel isolating. But it's the only way to ensure that your ideas will still matter when the noise has passed.

There is a misconception that legacy work must be long, academic, or dense. That's not true. Some of the most enduring works are deceptively simple. A poem. A question. A diagram. What defines legacy is not form, but function. It's whether the work creates a shift. Whether it alters someone's orientation to the world. Whether it provides language or structure that was previously missing. Whether it becomes reference material, not for one conversation, but for many.

To create this kind of work, you must also be willing to decenter yourself. Legacy is not built on personal branding. It's built on contribution. The best legacy work often becomes detached from its author. It circulates independently. It becomes part of the intellectual infrastructure of a field, a movement, a generation. And while that may bruise the ego, your name might not always travel with the idea; it strengthens the work. Because the work is no longer tethered to your visibility. It has legs of its own.

This decentering does not mean disappearing. It means shifting the emphasis from visibility to viability. You're not trying to be seen all the time. You're trying to make something that keeps working even when you're not talking about it. That is the real test of legacy: whether your absence diminishes the idea, or whether the concept continues to grow without you.

And when that happens, you begin to experience a different kind of creative freedom. You are no longer creating for the cycle. You are no longer beholden to the tyranny of the new. You can step away without fear of being forgotten. You can work in seasons, not sprints. You can invest in a single idea for years without feeling irrelevant because you've built something durable enough to withstand your silence.

That durability is what most creators never achieve, not because it's unattainable, but because it's unfamiliar. The platforms have trained us to equate relevance with immediacy, to believe that if we're not producing, we're disappearing. But that's a platform myth, not a creative truth. Some of the most impactful voices in history disappeared for decades at a time. They withdrew. They wandered. They reemerged when they had something new to offer. And their audiences waited, not because they were constantly visible, but because their absence felt like a pause, not an end.

In a disposable culture, to make people wait is radical. It signals that your work is not a product of pressure, but of purpose. It's worth the time it takes to make and receive. And when the audience begins to adopt that rhythm, a transformation occurs. The relationship shifts. They no longer expect constant stimulation. They begin to respect silence. They begin to value patience. They start to trust that what's coming is worth staying for.

And in that space, real impact is born.

Legacy, ultimately, is not about being remembered. It's about having made something worth remembering. There's a crucial difference. The first is ego-driven; the second is contribution-driven. When creators conflate the two, they chase attention in the name of legacy, and in doing so, often create nothing lasting. They build mirrors instead of tools, reflections of themselves instead of instruments others can use. But legacy is a tool. It is something that, once created, becomes useful to others. It helps people think, act, and decide. It survives not because of its author's name, but because of its utility. And that is what we should aim for, not to be celebrated, but to be useful.

In this sense, legacy work often looks deceptively modest from the outside. It doesn't always dominate the discourse. It doesn't always come with fanfare. Sometimes it lives quietly, until suddenly, it doesn't. Until someone finds it, uses it, shares it. And then, slowly, it spreads, not with the speed of gossip, but with the gravity of insight. That spread is not explosive, but expansive. It doesn't burn bright and vanish. It smolders, it travels, it endures.

Endurance is what the disposable culture cannot offer. The system isn't designed for it. Algorithms reward performance, not permanence. Platforms reward frictionless novelty, not the slow, uneasy friction of truth. And most creators internalize this without even realizing it. They begin to prioritize shareability over substance. They measure success by surface-level signals. They confuse frequency with relevance. And they forget that all of it — the likes, the reach, the clicks — can be wiped out with a single change in policy or platform direction.

Legacy work exists outside that fragility. It has roots. It doesn't need the algorithm to breathe. It can live in a book, in a classroom, in a framework, in a movement. It can be passed from person to person, offline, and untracked. It can be quoted in boardrooms, cited in research, whispered in moments of decision. It can resurface years later, when the world has caught up to its clarity. And when it does, it doesn't feel old. It feels essential.

This is the paradox: to create something timeless, you often have to ignore the times, not in arrogance, but in discipline. You have to resist the urge to react immediately. You have to tune out the noise of what's trending. You have to believe that your attention is better spent cultivating depth than capturing attention. And you have to protect that belief, because everything around you will conspire to shake it. The metrics. The feedback. The silence. The success of others. All of it will whisper the same message: speed up, fit in, keep posting.

But you don't have to listen.

Instead, you can create on a different wavelength. One that values coherence over cadence. One that allows ideas to ferment before they are shared. One that treats the audience not as consumers, but as collaborators in meaning-making. Because legacy is not built through consumption, it is built through participation. People don't carry your work forward because they liked it. They take it because it has become a part of how they think. Because they saw themselves in it. Because it was named something they hadn't been able to articulate. That is the kind of influence that transcends format. That is the kind of relevance that doesn't expire.

This is the final distinction: disposable content is consumed. Legacy work is integrated. One disappears when the scroll ends. The other lingers, reshaping the landscape long after the initial encounter. If you want to create that kind of work, you must begin with the assumption that it is possible. Although the culture might be loud and distracted, it remains hungry for substance. That people might skim now, but that doesn't mean they are incapable of depth. That attention might be fleeting, but understanding can still be pursued. You have to believe that the conditions for legacy still exist, even if they are rare, even if they are difficult to reach.

And then you must act accordingly.

You must write things that take longer to understand but are harder to forget. You must resist the temptation to dilute your ideas to fit the feed. You must be willing to be invisible, for a time, in service of becoming indispensable later. You must trust the arc of quality, even when it's quiet. You must build with care, not just speed. You must make things that are not just interesting, but inevitable.

That is how legacy begins, not with an audience, but with an orientation. Not with virality, but with vision. Not with visibility, but with voice.

And in a culture that has trained us to discard and replace, to scroll and forget, to mimic and perform, the act of building something to last is more than a creative decision. It is an act of resistance.

Chapter Eleven: Building an Ecosystem, Not an Audience

The prevailing wisdom in digital spaces is that the audience is everything. Build it, grow it, monetize it. Accumulate as many followers, subscribers, impressions, and page views as possible, and you'll have the leverage you need to thrive. That logic is drilled into every aspiring creator from the moment they post their first piece of content. But what's rarely examined is the fragility of this arrangement. An audience, no matter how large, is not a stable foundation. It is a rental agreement with attention to detail. And attention, as we've established, is fleeting, fickle, and heavily mediated by algorithms you don't control.

An audience can leave. It can be redirected. The whims of a platform update or a change in trend can reshape it. You can go from thousands of likes to silence overnight. You can have one misstep, one algorithmic penalty, one shift in platform culture, and the audience you've spent years building suddenly no longer sees you. It's not that they've turned on you; it's that the system has rerouted their gaze. If all you've built is an audience, then what you've built is vulnerable.

What you need instead is an ecosystem.

An ecosystem is not simply a group of followers. It's a resilient network of relationships, platforms, tools, rituals, and shared language. It's a dynamic, self-sustaining environment where ideas, values, and participation circulate. It's not predicated on passive consumption, but on active engagement. And unlike an audience, which exists primarily to watch, an ecosystem exists to contribute, to connect, and to reinforce itself over time.

The shift from audience to ecosystem changes how you build. It changes how you publish, how you speak, and how you organize your time. Audience-building prioritizes content velocity: more posts, more frequency, more touchpoints. Ecosystem-building prioritizes coherence: clearer ideas, stronger nodes, deeper connections. In an audience model, you win by being everywhere. In an ecosystem model, you win by creating places that are worth returning to.

This shift is not just semantic. It requires an entirely different architecture of presence. In an audience model, you optimize for broadcast, getting your message to as many people as possible. In an ecosystem, you optimize for circulation by designing touchpoints where people can engage with your work on multiple levels, in various formats, over time. That might mean long-form essays, followed by podcast interviews, followed by intimate community forums. It might mean recurring newsletters, private workshops, or co-created frameworks. The point is not just to be heard. It's to create an environment where your ideas can evolve and deepen through repeated exposure and interaction.

Ecosystem thinking also transforms your relationship to platforms. You stop being loyal to any single one. You use them as tools, not homes. You publish where your audience happens to be, but you always aim to bring them into a space you own, such as a mailing list, a membership site, or a publication you control. You build redundancy into your strategy. You assume disruption will come. And because you've built something more profound than a feed, it doesn't collapse when the platform falters.

Creators who build ecosystems tend to think differently about scale. They understand that a smaller, engaged, invested network is more powerful than a large, passive one. They stop chasing vanity metrics. They start focusing on density, how many people are not just seeing the work, but using it, sharing it, applying it. And because their work is structurally integrated into the lives of their audience, their influence becomes less visible but more durable. They are not trending; they are embedded.

This model of embedded influence is what allows creators to make long-term bets. They can launch a book, not to strangers, but to a network that has already internalized their ideas. They can run an event and fill the room with people who speak their language. They can experiment with new formats, trusting that their ecosystem will adapt with them. That adaptability is what makes the ecosystem so powerful; it evolves as you evolve. You're not locked into a single format, voice, or persona. You have room to grow, because the system is not built on novelty. It's built on trust.

Trust is the currency of ecosystems. Not engagement. Not clicks. Not reach. Trust. And trust, once earned, cannot be replaced by an ad budget. It is the product of showing up consistently, saying something worth hearing, and honoring the people who choose to stay. It's not about manipulating behavior; it's about building reliability. People come back not because they were tricked into clicking, but because they know they'll find clarity, coherence, or connection.

In this way, ecosystems humanize the work. They move the creator out of the spotlight and into the network. They shift the goal from attention to contribution. They create the conditions for dialogue, not just dissemination. And perhaps most importantly, they allow for resilience, not just in the face of platform change, but in the face of personal change. You are not forced to keep performing to remain relevant. You can step back. You can evolve. And your ecosystem, if it's well-designed, will not vanish. It will wait.

Stepping back becomes not a risk, but a rhythm. The ecosystem doesn't punish silence the way audiences conditioned by algorithms might. It doesn't assume absence equals abandonment. It understands that seasons of visible output alternate with seasons of invisible cultivation. Some of your most meaningful work will happen offstage, refining an idea, researching a new direction, rethinking your values. The ecosystem holds space for that process. It trusts that when you return, what you bring will be worth the wait.

This trust is built slowly. It begins with how you invite people into your world. Do you lure them in with spectacle, only to deliver nothing of substance? Or do you greet them with clarity, depth, and a clear sense of purpose? The entry point matters. Because ecosystems grow through alignment, not hype, people stay when they recognize something familiar, not just in your message, but in your mindset. They stay when your work helps them see themselves more clearly. They remain when the value is not just intellectual, but emotional, even moral. They stay when they sense you're building something with them, not just at them.

This "withness" is essential. Ecosystems are not fan clubs. They are networks of mutual utility. The creator is not a performer, and the audience is not a crowd. Everyone has a role to play. Everyone brings something to the table. Some ask questions. Some remix your ideas. Some build adjacent projects. Some show up and make your work part of their thinking. The result is not a one-way funnel; it's a multi-threaded network. And that network doesn't just amplify your message. It refines it. Strengthens it. Pressure-test it. Turns it into something that can survive outside of you.

When this happens, your work stops being content and starts becoming culture, not in the broad, influencer sense of "pop culture," but in the precise, grounded sense of shared practices, shared language, and shared norms. You're no longer just publishing ideas; you're helping shape a worldview. You're not just building followers, you're enabling a way of seeing, of doing, of being. And that shift, when people begin to recognize themselves through the lens of your work, is what turns an ecosystem from an audience alternative into a force multiplier.

Force multipliers don't just expand your reach. They deepen your impact. A well-designed ecosystem means you don't have to be the only one talking. Others carry your ideas forward. They bring your frameworks into new industries. They adapt your principles to different communities. They cite you, yes, but more importantly, they build on you. They extend the lineage. And because ecosystems are regenerative by nature, this extension doesn't dilute your influence; it magnifies it.

But to allow for this, you have to let go of total control. You cannot manage every expression of your work. You cannot dictate how people interpret or evolve your ideas. You must learn to distinguish between integrity and ownership. Protecting the integrity of your work means maintaining its core clarity, ensuring that your ideas are not misrepresented, distorted, or stripped of nuance. But it does not mean clinging to authorship. It does not mean blocking adaptation. Legacy work, as discussed before, becomes truly powerful when it detaches from ego. Ecosystem work follows the same logic: your impact grows as your grip loosens.

That's why ecosystems thrive on documentation. You must make your thinking accessible, not just through finished content, but through visible process. Let people see how you arrived at an idea. Let them understand the questions you asked, the sources you consulted, and the patterns you noticed. When you expose your method, you give others a framework they can use. You stop being just a source of information. You become a node of orientation. And that is far more valuable.

Documentation also future-proofs your work. Ideas that live only in your head or on ephemeral platforms disappear with you. But when your ideas are codified, mapped, named, and shared, they can travel independently. They can find new homes. They can inspire other systems, other projects, other creators. You are not just building content. You are building infrastructure. And infrastructure, by design, endures.

Of course, this doesn't mean abandoning the platforms entirely. They are still valuable tools for discovery. But the difference is that you are no longer dependent on them. You use the algorithm to signal people toward the deeper parts of your world, but your real work happens elsewhere. The post is not the product. The feed is not the destination. It's the invitation.

And when someone accepts that invitation, they don't just consume, they enter. They move from the outside of your world to the inside. From follower to participant. From visitor to resident. That transition is the fundamental metric of success, not how many people saw your work, but how many decided to stay.

When someone stays, they begin to behave differently. They no longer scroll past your work the way they might with a stranger's content. They pause. They engage. They carry the conversation forward, sometimes without you. They bring others into the fold, not because you asked them to, but because they've found value they want to share. In this way, your ecosystem becomes more than a structure. It becomes a social fabric. A community of interpretation. A distributed intelligence. And it becomes less about you and more about the ideas that live through you.

This is where the myth of personal branding begins to dissolve. So many creators have been taught to build a brand around their personality, their lifestyle, their curated moments of authority. But personality-based branding, while seductive in the short term, rarely sustains in the long term. It requires constant performance. Constant presence. It positions the creator as the product. And over time, that positioning becomes a trap. You can't change without risking dissonance. You can't rest without risking irrelevance. You can't evolve without potentially mastering the very identity your brand was built on.

Ecosystems offer a different model. They allow you to lead with values, with vision, with frameworks. They allow your identity to evolve because the work is not tethered to your performance; it's tethered to the clarity of your thinking. The ecosystem doesn't collapse if your tone changes or your face disappears. It continues because it was never about spectacle. It was about coherence. It was about building something that mattered to others on terms they could live with, think with, and grow with.

This shift also changes the nature of creative responsibility. When you have an audience, your main task is to deliver value. When you have an ecosystem, your task expands. You are not just providing content. You are stewarding space. You are setting norms. You are shaping culture. And while that may sound lofty, it's also practical. Because when people enter your world, they are not just consuming ideas; they are adopting postures. Toward attention. Toward complexity. Toward each other. And how you structure your ecosystem will determine the quality of those postures.

Structure is everything. It's not enough to have good content. You must think like an architect. Where do people enter? How do they move through your world? What signals do they encounter along the way? What paths are visible? Which are hidden? Where do they stop and reflect? Where do they contribute? Where do they deepen their commitment? These are not just UX questions. They are cultural ones. Because how you design the journey shapes what the journey produces.

A well-designed ecosystem creates outcomes that a simple audience never could. It surfaces emergent behavior. It catalyzes ideas you never planned. It becomes self-expanding. Someone reads your essay, creates a tool from it, hosts a workshop, and invites others to participate. Someone hears your podcast, integrates your model into their framework, and attributes it forward. Someone watches your talk and begins to rethink their entire approach to their work. And you are not managing any of this. You are just tending the garden. Making sure the conditions remain fertile.

This is the real freedom creators crave. Not the illusion of passive income. Not the dopamine of viral attention. But the deeper freedom of knowing that your work has a life beyond you. That it will continue to move, evolve, and contribute even when you're offline, or offstage, or just off. Because the system isn't held together by your energy alone, it's held together by shared value. Shared understanding. Shared ownership.

To build something like this requires a rejection of the dominant logic. You have to stop thinking in terms of funnels and follower counts. You have to stop viewing people as leads or as numbers in a dashboard. You have to rehumanize your process. To remember that what you are doing is not engineering behavior, but instead building relationships—both with individuals and with an idea, a mission, and a vision of what could be possible when attention is treated with care.

The irony is that ecosystems, though harder to build, are often what audiences wanted all along. People don't crave more content. They crave connection. They crave places to think aloud. To be heard. To grow. To wrestle with ideas that don't fit neatly into a caption. The creators who provide that space, who build not just for reach, but for resonance, become irreplaceable. Not because they're loud, but because they're real. Not because they have all the answers, but because they've built somewhere worth returning to.

And in a culture that is constantly demanding that we move faster, post more, shout louder, to build somewhere worth returning to is perhaps the most radical act of all.

Chapter Twelve: Designing for Depth

Depth has become a kind of rebellion. In a digital culture shaped by speed and saturated with stimuli, to go deep, to linger, to question, to resist the urge to respond immediately, is to act against the grain. The systems we operate in are engineered for immediacy. They reward the quick take, the emotional spike, the content that can be consumed without reflection and discarded without loss. Platforms prioritize what is easy to share, not what is challenging to sit with. And so creators, even those with good intentions, begin to bend their work toward the shallow end of the pool.

They do it to stay visible. To keep up. To meet the assumed expectations of an audience they've never met. And slowly, often without noticing, they trade depth for legibility. They simplify their ideas, not for clarity, but for speed. They strip out the nuance, not to sharpen their message, but to ensure the algorithm doesn't bury it. They begin to craft not from intention, but from reaction, what will get picked up, what will go viral, what won't be misunderstood if skimmed. And in doing so, they become trapped in the very system they hoped to transcend.

But there is another way. It begins with a simple shift: stop designing for reach and start planning for resonance. Resonance is what happens when your work doesn't just pass through someone's feed but settles in their mind. It's what makes someone return to an idea days later, unprompted. It's what makes a phrase stick, a metaphor circulate, a question reappear in moments of decision. And resonance cannot be manufactured through volume. It requires depth. It requires the courage to say less but mean more. To prioritize what lasts over what lands.

To design for depth means to take your audience seriously, not as passive consumers of information, but as people capable of complexity. It means trusting them with ambiguity. It means creating space for reflection, not just reaction. It means building ideas that require a second read, a pause, a conversation. Not because they are obscure or convoluted, but because they are rich. Because they contain layers. Because they are designed not to impress, but to unfold.

This unfolding doesn't happen in isolation. It requires an environment, one that supports slowness, attention, and meaningful repetition. It might begin with a piece of writing, but it extends through the rhythms you establish around that writing. Do you publish so often that no single idea has time to land? Do you create rituals that encourage your audience to return and re-engage? Do you offer moments of quiet in a culture that never stops shouting?

These aren't questions of style; they are questions of design. Because depth is not just about content, it's about context. The same idea can feel shallow or profound depending on how it is delivered. A complex thought delivered at high speed, surrounded by noise, loses its weight. But slow it down, isolate it, let it breathe, and it begins to take on gravity. That's the work of the designer. To create not just what is said, but the conditions under which it can be heard.

This is where many creators fall short. They spend all their energy on refining the message, but little on shaping the environment in which the message will live. They assume the content will speak for itself. But in a shallow system, depth needs scaffolding. It needs protection. It needs to be framed, supported, and guided. Otherwise, it gets flattened and reduced to a soundbite. Misread. Ignored. Or worse, repurposed for a goal it was never intended to serve.

Scaffolding might mean the way you open a piece, do you rush into the point, or do you build the terrain slowly? It might mean the length; do you allow enough space for the idea to develop, or do you compress it into something that fits the feed? It might mean the medium, some ideas need to be spoken, others drawn, and others written. Choosing the wrong one can make even the most profound thought feel weightless.

But more than anything, designing for depth requires you to step out of the pace the culture demands. You have to create from a different rhythm. You have to resist the sense that if it's not published today, it doesn't matter. You have to honor the time an idea needs to mature, not just for you, but for the people who will receive it. Because depth is not just about what you say, it's about when it's heard. A perfectly constructed insight delivered too early will still be dismissed. The same insight, delivered when the audience is ready, can reshape their thinking.

This timing cannot be gamed. It can only be sensed. And that sense only sharpens when you stop looking at metrics and start listening to momentum. What are people struggling with? What questions keep surfacing? What patterns are you noticing that others haven't named yet? These are signals of readiness, not for content, but for clarity. And clarity, delivered at the right moment, is what creates impact that doesn't evaporate.

Clarity, when shaped properly, becomes a vessel. It carries not only meaning, but presence. And in a digital world that is constantly vying for our fragmented attention, presence is power. A clear thought, expressed in a moment of noise, has the rare ability to stop the scroll, not because it's loud, but because it's whole. People sense when something has been thoroughly considered. They may not articulate it that way, but they feel it. It lands differently. It asks something of them. It invites them not to consume, but to enter.

To create that kind of clarity, you have to go beyond surface-level understanding. You have to become intimate with your ideas. Not just what you believe, but why you believe it. Not just what the message is, but what it's about. And that means spending time beneath the surface, questioning, rewriting, stripping away the ornamental in pursuit of the essential. The goal is not to impress your audience. It is to meet them. To offer them something so grounded, so intentional, that it quiets the noise around it by sheer contrast.

But quiet work is rarely rewarded in the short term. Platforms are not optimized for stillness. They amplify what provokes. What distracts. What confirms existing bias. Depth, by contrast, often disrupts. It introduces ambiguity. It resists binary framing. It complicates the narrative. And so it doesn't always perform well at first glance. It might get fewer shares, fewer likes. It might even be ignored by the systems you've been trained to serve. This is where most creators falter, not because their work lacks substance, but because they misread the silence as failure.

Silence is not failure. In the context of deep work, silence is often the precondition for significance. It's the space in which meaning settles. When someone reads something profound, they don't always respond immediately. Sometimes they pause. They reflect. They carry it with them into a conversation days later. They don't react because the idea didn't ask for a reaction; it asked for attention. That attention might not be visible in metrics, but it is palpable in memory. It becomes a reference point, a tool, a shift in worldview. That's the kind of impact numbers can't quantify.

And so the challenge is to stay the course. To keep creating for depth even when the feedback loops go quiet. To resist the impulse to simplify in the name of shareability. To refuse to flatten your ideas just to fit the screen. Your job is not to be popular in the moment, but to be useful over time. To offer clarity when the fog lifts. To be the signal others come back to when the noise becomes unbearable.

One way to do this is to anchor your work in questions rather than answers. Questions have a unique staying power. A well-posed question can travel farther than any confident claim. It can open a line of inquiry that lives beyond the bounds of your platform. It can lodge itself in someone's thinking and shape the way they approach an entirely different conversation—answers close loops. Questions open them. And opening loops is what invites people into depth.

But this requires humility. You have to let go of the need always to be right. You have to let your ideas evolve in public. You have to risk not being understood immediately. And you have to be okay with the fact that your deepest work might not be appreciated until long after it's published. That's not failure. That's timing. Some ideas arrive before the culture is ready to receive them. Your job is not to force the reception. It's to prepare the ground.

Preparation also means cultivating your internal environment. If you're constantly chasing metrics, if you're optimizing every decision for reach, you will not be able to hear what your work is trying to become. You'll shape it to please others instead of allowing it to guide you. Depth demands solitude. It demands stillness. It demands a willingness to sit with discomfort. Not every insight will arrive fully formed. Some will arrive tangled. Some will arrive incomplete. Some will resist articulation for weeks, months, or even years. But if you honor their pace, if you give them the space to unfold, they will reward you with clarity.

And when that clarity arrives, everything else begins to organize around it. Your structure becomes obvious. Your tone becomes natural. Your message becomes undeniable, not because it's loud, but because it's true. You don't need to yell when what you're saying is real. You don't need to hype what already resonates. You need to make space for the right people to find it, in the right moment, in the right frame of mind.

Depth is not for everyone. And that's precisely the point. When you design for depth, you are not creating for the masses. You are creating for those who are ready to go further. You are filtering, not in the traditional marketing sense of segmentation or demographics, but in the philosophical sense. You are choosing to speak in a way that may not be heard by all, but will be felt more deeply by those who do listen to it. You are building not just an audience, but a fellowship of thinkers, readers, builders, skeptics, and seers—people who are tired of noise and are hungry for substance.

This is not a scarcity play. It is a rich play. You are not trying to reach everyone. You are trying to matter deeply to the few who are willing to do the work with you. And when you build that kind of relationship, you begin to tap into a different kind of creative fuel. You stop chasing affirmation from the crowd and start drawing energy from resonance. You feel less pressure to perform and more freedom to explore. You no longer need to be prolific to feel productive. A single piece, written with clarity and received with seriousness, becomes more meaningful than a dozen optimized posts.

But meaning is not passive. It must be constructed. And the construction of meaning takes time. Time to read. Time to reflect. Time to return. In a culture that devalues duration, your job as a creator is to insist on it. To design your work in a way that resists premature consumption. To create entry points that slow people down. To build in pauses, digressions, spaces that ask not just "Did you get it?" but "Have you lived with it yet?"

This might mean changing the way you format your writing, the way you deliver your talks, or the way you structure your courses. It might mean creating companion pieces, reflections, exercises, and provocations that encourage digestion. It might mean mastering a single idea into multiple touchpoints, giving people the opportunity to encounter it more than once, in more than one way. Because repetition, in a shallow environment, is an act of care. It says: This is worth hearing again. This is worth getting right.

And when people feel that kind of care, when they sense that your work was designed not just to grab their attention, but to respect it, they respond differently. They give you more attention in return. They open up more. They share more. They integrate your ideas more fully. They come back, not because an algorithm is pushing them, but because they are being pulled by meaning.

That pull is what every serious creator wants, whether they articulate it or not. Not just reach. Not just visibility. But a kind of gravitational presence. A sense that the work is not just momentarily interesting, but permanently relevant. A sense that what's being said matters, not because of trend alignment, but because of inner alignment. And that alignment, once felt, is not easily forgotten. People remember where they were when they read something that made them stop. They remember the moment when a vague unease found its name. They remember the source that didn't just speak to them, but saw them.

This is what depth can do. It creates memory. It creates movement. It creates work that doesn't just live in a feed, but in a life. And that kind of work does not fade when the algorithm changes. It does not evaporate when the metrics dip. It does not need to be shouted from the rooftops every week to stay relevant. It becomes part of how people perceive and decide, how they relate to the world. That is the mark of truly enduring creative labor. It rewires perception.

But to create something that rewires perception, you must first be willing to resist your conditioning. You must unlearn the reflex to please the algorithm. You must slow down your output. You must deepen your input. You must listen to yourself long enough to discern what is real from what is reactive. And you must trust, perhaps unthinkingly at first, that the people who need this depth will find it. That they are out there, scrolling through noise, waiting to be interrupted by something that finally makes them feel seen.

Designing for depth in a shallow environment is not a strategy. It is a stance. It is a commitment to integrity in the face of volatility. It is a quiet refusal to believe that everything must be faster, louder, shorter, simpler. It is a declaration that some things are still worth the time. Still worth the effort. Still worth getting right.

And in making that declaration, not with slogans, but with the quality of your work, you become not just a creator, but a guide. Not just a voice, but a presence. Not just a node in the network, but a landmark in someone's thinking.

That's not content.

That's craft.

Chapter Thirteen: When the Work Speaks for You

There comes a point in every creator's trajectory when the work must take on a life of its own. Not metaphorically, not aspirationally, but functionally. A moment when the attention shifts from the maker to the made. When what you've built becomes capable of standing, without your constant narration, without your presence on stage, without your daily efforts to prop it up. This isn't abdication. It's the necessary maturation of serious work. If the work is good enough, coherent enough, and grounded sufficiently, it will begin to speak for itself.

But this is a difficult transition. Most creators never get there. Not because they aren't capable, but because they don't let go. They remain tethered to the spotlight, convinced that visibility is the only safeguard against irrelevance. They assume that stepping back means slipping away. So they keep posting, keep explaining, keep managing the narrative. And in doing so, they undermine the very authority they're trying to build. They become performers of expertise, rather than architects of something lasting.

The truth is, if you have to keep explaining your value, your value isn't clear. At least not yet. And that's not a marketing problem; it's a design problem. Work that truly speaks for you doesn't need to beg for attention. It earns it through substance. It doesn't need to demand loyalty. It cultivates it through usefulness. And it doesn't fade when you step out of frame. It continues because it has structure, intention, and resonance baked in.

When the work speaks, it reaches people you'll never meet. It enters rooms you'll never walk into. It finds its way into conversations, presentations, boardrooms, and classrooms. Not because it's viral, but because it's valuable. Not because it was gamed for distribution, but because it offers something others can carry forward. And that is the point, work that speaks for you is work that can travel without you.

This requires a shift in how we think about authorship. In the early stages of creation, your name matters. It's how people find you. It's how trust is established. But over time, if the work is good, your name should matter less. The idea becomes the thing. The framework becomes what gets repeated. The phrase, the question, and the lens start to circulate on their own. This is not a loss of identity. It is a transfer of attention from the person to the principle.

That transfer is a sign of maturity, not erasure. It means the work has reached a point of independence. It no longer relies on your performance to stay alive. It has its coherence. Its credibility. Others have internalized it and adapted, referenced, and built upon it. It no longer needs to be defended. It can stand in the face of critique. It can be misinterpreted and still survive. That is how you know the work is real.

But honest work like this is rare and hard. It is not built on charisma. It is built on clarity. It is not built on aesthetics. It is built on function. And it is not measured by reach, but by influence. Influence that shows up not in likes or shares, but in how your work changes the way others think. The way they speak. The way they structure their systems. When your job starts showing up in other people's frameworks, not just as a citation but as a building block, that's when you know it's speaking.

Of course, getting to this point takes time. It takes patience. It takes a relentless commitment to coherence. You have to be willing to refine an idea until it's clean enough to replicate and sturdy enough to survive without your voice next to it. You have to design your work like a tool, simple on the surface, deep in function, adaptable in application. That doesn't mean dumbing it down. It means stripping away the noise until what remains is essential. And then stress-testing that essence. Making sure it holds.

This process is invisible to most. All they see is the finished product, the framework that spreads, the concept that gets quoted, the book that gets passed around. What they don't see is the dozens of drafts, the hours of conversation, the quiet moments of doubt. They don't know the work that went into making the work speak. And they shouldn't have to. Because the work, when it's doing its job, speaks for itself.

There is a kind of quiet authority in work that speaks without spectacle. It doesn't rely on urgency. It doesn't need the push of marketing gimmicks or the bait of sensational headlines. It stands because it was built with unquestionable integrity. It was not rushed into relevance; it was crafted with intention. That's what gives it weight. That's what gives it staying power. It's the difference between a trend and a touchstone. One flickers and fades. The other becomes part of how people orient themselves.

And orientation is the actual test. When your work begins to function as a compass for others, helping them navigate their uncertainty, make better decisions, see their patterns more clearly, that's when you've moved beyond influence and into legacy. Not legacy in the ego-driven, name-etched-on-buildings sense. But legacy is in the quiet, cumulative way that fundamental ideas spread. Someone reads your essay and makes a better hiring decision. Someone hears your interview and redesigns their client onboarding process. Someone uses your metaphor in a high-stakes negotiation. That's not clout. That's utility.

And utility is the most overlooked metric in a culture obsessed with visibility. Visibility can be gamed. It can be bought, borrowed, or stolen. But utility? That must be earned. And it's usually invisible at first. No one throws a parade for the idea that helps someone frame a complicated conversation. No chart tracks the concept that shifted someone's approach to time, leadership, or creative risk. But those shifts, those invisible, private, personal adaptations, are where your work starts to embed itself in real life. That's where it begins to matter.

Creators who aim for this kind of embeddedness understand that they are not building content; they are building infrastructure. They're not just filling feeds; they're creating tools, frameworks, and language that other people can use. They know that a well-designed phrase can do more than a viral post. A clear diagram can unlock more insight than a thousand wordy blog updates. They optimize not for volume, but for velocity of application, how quickly and deeply the work can be used, adapted, and internalized.

To build for use rather than applause requires a different kind of ego. One who is comfortable being absent. One that doesn't need constant credit. One that is satisfied knowing the work is working, even if no one's tagging you in the results. It's not that recognition doesn't matter. It's that it's not the point. The point is to build something that can travel farther than you can. And to do that, you often have to step aside.

Stepping aside doesn't mean disappearing. It means designing systems that don't require your constant intervention. It means making your work portable, able to be shared, reused, and explained by others. It means thinking not like a performer, but like a systems builder. What structures will this idea live in? What supports will help it scale? What language will help it land, and what redundancies will help it stay intact under stress? These are not questions creators are often taught to ask. But they are the questions that turn good work into enduring work.

And enduring work is what ultimately reshapes culture. Not through volume, but through persistence. Not through spectacle, but through structure. When your ideas become part of how people operate, when they're cited in onboarding decks, woven into therapy sessions, mapped onto business models, you are no longer just a creator. You are an architect of mental models. A builder of interpretive tools. A contributor to how people make sense of their world.

That kind of contribution doesn't announce itself. It reveals itself gradually. You begin to hear your words echoed back to you in conversations with strangers. You start to see people teaching your ideas, adapting your diagrams, evolving your metaphors. And you realize they don't need you in the room for your work to do its job. That's not the end of relevance. That's the proof of it.

It's also the freedom you've been seeking. Because when the work speaks for you, you no longer have to scream. You no longer have to stay online 24/7. You no longer have to promote your presence with content constantly. The work is out there, doing its job. Your name might be mentioned. It might not. But either way, the influence remains because you built something that lasts.

To reach that place of quiet influence requires discipline, the discipline to build slowly, and to resist the reflex to announce your progress constantly. In the early days, it's easy to fall into the trap of validation-seeking. You want to know if the work is landing, so you push it out prematurely, test it too often, and dilute it before it's ready. You chase engagement because you've been conditioned to believe that feedback equals value. But the deepest work grows in silence, shielded from public scrutiny until it's strong enough to withstand it. Some of your most crucial thinking will happen in private, in notebooks, in half-finished drafts, in conversations with no witnesses. And that's as it should be.

Mature creators learn to protect that early stage. They don't confuse exposure with progress. They understand that the right ideas need incubation. That forcing clarity too soon leads to brittle conclusions. What matters is not how quickly an idea can be published, but how well it holds up when it finally enters the world. They resist the pressure to package, constantly post, constantly prove, constantly. Because they are building for something bigger than the algorithm's momentary approval, they are building something that can be returned to.

Returnability is a concept we rarely discuss, but it's central to the kind of work that speaks for you. Anyone can create content that captures attention for a moment. But how many creators can say their job is re-read? Revisited? Quoted a year later in a completely different context? That kind of durability doesn't happen by accident. It happens when you prioritize structure, clarity, and substance over speed and spectacle. It happens when you treat your output not as an expression, but as a construction, something built to bear weight.

That weight is what gives your work presence even when you're not around to explain it. An obvious idea doesn't need the author's charisma to be understood. A well-drawn framework doesn't need a webinar to function. A resonant phrase doesn't need your social media strategy to circulate. These things live because they've been crafted with autonomy in mind. They're not dependent on your performance. They're designed to survive distribution.

And when you shift into that mode, when you stop thinking like a performer and start thinking like a builder, you begin to experience a new kind of creative satisfaction. One that isn't tied to likes or follows. One that doesn't vanish when the algorithm changes. One that emerges from the simple, quiet knowledge that your work is functioning in the world. That it's doing its job, without constant input from you. That it's alive.

But here's the paradox: for your work to reach that level of independence, you must first be completely inside it. You must obsess over the details. You must make peace with the long cycle. You must do the work of clarifying every layer, every assumption, every mechanism. You must test the edges of your ideas, name the boundaries, and anticipate the misunderstandings. It's an exhausting process. And it's invisible to almost everyone. But it's what allows the final product to appear effortless, obvious, and self-evident.

That self-evidence is what makes others say, "This makes sense," even if they can't explain why. It's what makes your frameworks feel like common sense after the fact. It's what gives your ideas the ring of truth, even to people encountering them for the first time. And that sense of obviousness is not a sign that your work was simplistic. It's a sign that your complexity was well-contained. That your structure was doing its job.

Structure is what turns insight into infrastructure. It's what transforms personal clarity into public utility. And it's what allows your work to become part of how others think, even when your name is no longer attached to it. That's not invisibility. That's legacy. Because what's remembered is not the branding. It's not the headline. It's the shift that the work created. The crack opened. The direction it pointed to.

When you reach that level, when your work is traveling further than you are, you start to understand what influence means. Not the illusion of reach, but the reality of integration. Not visibility for its own sake, but visibility that enables new action, new thought, new connection. And you realize: this was never about being famous. It was about being useful. Enduringly, invisibly, usefully present in the minds and methods of others.

In a world that tells you to shout louder, to post more, to chase every trend, choosing instead to build work that speaks for you is not just rare, it's radical. It's a way of resisting the erosion of attention. It's a way of honoring the reader. It's a way of leaving a mark that doesn't wash away when the feed refreshes. And in the end, it may be the only kind of influence that matters.

Chapter Fourteen: Making Peace with the Plateau

There's a moment in every creative or strategic endeavor when the momentum slows. Not because you've made a mistake, not because you've lost your edge, but because growth has found its limit, for now. It's the plateau. That long, flat stretch where progress isn't apparent and praise isn't pouring in. Where the numbers stall, where the spark that fueled the early work feels like it's been replaced with silence, for creators conditioned to expect linear results, this moment feels like failure. But it isn't. It's simply the middle. And the middle is where the real work begins.

The culture doesn't talk about this. Platforms and pundits glorify the launch, the spike, the viral moment. They fetishize the early ascent, when followers multiply, comments flood in, and opportunities seem to appear from nowhere. But few talk about what happens after the surge, when the novelty fades, when the audience stabilizes. When the algorithm seems to look elsewhere, that phase, the plateau, is rarely acknowledged and rarely celebrated. And yet, it is where most enduring work is made.

Because the plateau is not the absence of progress, it is the terrain of refinement. It is the space where clarity deepens, systems mature, and substance replaces spectacle. It's where you begin to separate performance from practice. Anyone can create with momentum at their back. But to make it when the applause has quieted, when the metrics don't validate you, when the market seems distracted, that requires discipline. It involves belief in the process, not just in the outcomes. And that belief must be earned, not assumed.

Making peace with the plateau starts with rethinking what growth looks like. Growth is not always external. Sometimes it is subterranean. Sometimes the most important changes are invisible to the eye but vital to the work. You refine your voice. You clarify your frameworks. You deepen your research. You start to see connections you missed when you were racing to keep up. This is growth that doesn't trend. But it transforms. And in the long arc of a creative career, it matters more than any single viral moment.

But to embrace this kind of growth, you have to resist the panic. The panic that tells you something is wrong. That if you're not growing fast, you're shrinking. That if you're not posting often, you're forgotten. That if the numbers aren't climbing, you've become irrelevant. These are lies, cultural distortions born of a system that equates visibility with value. But your work is not a brand. Your ideas are not campaigns. And your creative rhythm is not a product launch.

This is where many creators burn out. They confuse momentum with meaning. They become addicted to acceleration. And when the acceleration stops, as it always does, they assume something must be broken. So they push harder. Post more. Pivot into something louder. They chase the next spike instead of trusting the slope. And in doing so, they often erode the very foundation they were trying to build. The work becomes shallow. The ideas get rushed. The clarity fades. And what remains is noise, no different from everything else.

Sustainable work, on the other hand, requires patience. It requires the willingness to go quiet when the system says to stay loud. It requires you to keep showing up for work even when the world isn't watching. Because the plateau is not a verdict, it's a phase. And how you behave in that phase determines what comes next. If you treat it as a dead end, it becomes one. If you treat it as a studio, it becomes the place where your best ideas are born.

And often, they are. Without the pressure to constantly perform, you start to experiment again. You try things you wouldn't risk when the spotlight is brighter. You follow curiosity instead of metrics. You revisit old ideas and discover new angles. You write not to publish, but to understand. And in doing so, you rediscover the reason you began. Not to chase attention. But to make something that matters.

The plateau offers a unique kind of freedom, but only to those who are willing to stop grasping. When you're no longer chasing the high of rapid growth or viral traction, you can begin to evaluate your work on its terms. You start asking harder, more honest questions, not "How do I go bigger?" but "Is this even good?" Not "What will get the most clicks?" but "What does this mean?" These are the kinds of questions that don't get answered in the public arena. They get responded to in solitude. They get answered in the workshop of slow, deliberate effort.

And effort, in this phase, must become internalized. You are not performing for others. You are fortifying yourself. You are revisiting your assumptions, stress-testing your methods, and interrogating the weak links in your thinking. You are not trying to outshine anyone. You are trying to outlast yourself. That is a different kind of game, a longer one, a quieter one, and, often, a lonelier one. While the early stages of a creative career are typically social, full of support, feedback, and shared enthusiasm, the plateau can be isolating. Others have moved on. The novelty has worn off. And the discipline becomes yours alone to carry.

It is in this isolation, though, that endurance is formed. Endurance is not the ability to keep producing. It is the ability to keep caring. To stay emotionally invested in the work even when the world offers no reward. To keep refining your thinking even when no one's asking. Maintaining your standards is even more challenging when cutting corners would be easier. That kind of endurance is not built in moments of hype. It is built in moments of silence, when all you have is the question: "Why am I still doing this?"

Answering that question becomes the foundation for your next phase. Because if your answer is honest, if it's rooted not in status, but in service; not in ego, but in inquiry, then you begin to work from a deeper place. You stop seeking motivation and start cultivating conviction. Conviction that the work matters. Conviction that the process will pay off, even if you can't yet see how. Conviction that your job is not to impress, but to persist.

From this place, creativity becomes less fragile. You're no longer dependent on mood. You're not waiting for inspiration to strike. You've built habits that carry you. You've built scaffolding around your process. And perhaps most importantly, you've learned how to operate without applause. That ability, to work without external validation, is the secret strength behind every serious career. It's what allows you to keep showing up when others drift away. It's what makes your work more real. Not reactive. Not performative. Real.

This is not to say that recognition doesn't matter. We all want to be seen. We all want our efforts to be acknowledged. But when you've made peace with the plateau, you stop needing recognition to continue. You stop waiting for the spike to validate your worth. You realize that the work you're doing now, the slow, iterative, sometimes maddeningly quiet work, is what's setting you apart. Because very few people can do it. Very few can maintain momentum when the feedback is minimal. Very few can keep going when the metrics go mute.

But those who can? They become formidable. Because their work doesn't depend on fleeting attention, it doesn't evaporate when the algorithm shifts. It has roots. It has weight. It has staying power, not because it was hyped, but because it was built with integrity over time. The time that was spent on the plateau. The time that most others skipped.

So when you find yourself in that flat stretch, when your growth has slowed, when your audience seems dormant, when your engagement has plateaued, don't panic. Don't pivot. Don't abandon what you've built. Sit with it. Work through it. Use the silence to hear what your work is asking of you. And trust that what you create in this quiet season might be what shapes everything that comes next.

The plateau tests your maturity as a creator. It doesn't ask if you're talented. It asks if you're consistent. It doesn't care how loud your launch was. It wants to know what remains when the crowd stops clapping. This phase, more than any other, strips away the illusion that attention is the measure of worth. It reminds you that influence is not built in spikes. It's built into the decisions you make when no one is watching. Will you keep refining? Will you keep questioning? Will you continue to work on it, even when it doesn't perform?

This is where the myth of constant growth collapses. In a metrics-driven environment, we've been conditioned to believe that anything that isn't expanding must be shrinking. But that's not how deep systems work. In biology, in architecture, in relationships, growth often requires pauses, periods of apparent stasis where energy is redirected below the surface. Roots thicken. Foundations settle. Muscle repair. These phases don't show on charts. But they're necessary for anything meant to endure. Your creative practice is no different.

If you never allow for stillness, your structure becomes unsound. You grow wide, but not deep. Visible, but not grounded. Loud, but not lasting. The plateau is the invitation to fix that. It's the pause in the music that allows the melody to continue with more force. And if you can accept that, if you can stop resenting the lull and start working inside it, you'll begin to see that this period is not your enemy. It is your ally. Not a punishment, but a proving ground.

It is on the plateau that your systems reveal themselves. Systems are what sustain you when the spark dims. They are the routines, habits, and rituals that keep the work alive even when your energy fades. If you've built them well, they carry you. If you haven't, this is where the cracks show. And that's the gift of the plateau: it surfaces the weak points. It shows you where your strategy is brittle, where your voice is borrowed, and where your motivations are shallow. And it gives you time, precious, uninterrupted time, to rebuild.

Rebuilding here is not about dramatic reinvention. It's not a rebrand. It's not a pivot to whatever is trending. It's about strengthening the core and returning to the questions that first drove you. Not for nostalgia's sake, but for recalibration. What was I trying to say? Who am I saying it for? What's the impact I want this work to have? These questions, revisited from a quieter vantage point, often yield deeper answers. Because now you're not answering to impress. You're answering to understand.

And in that understanding, a kind of creative authority begins to form, not performative, not loud, but unmistakable. People can feel when the work is rooted. When it's no longer trying to prove itself. When it's being done for its own sake, and for the people it's meant to serve, not for the algorithm, not for vanity metrics, not for manufactured virality. That kind of work lands differently. It doesn't have to fight for space. It commands it.

This is how the plateau becomes not a pause, but a foundation. It gives you the room to build depth instead of breadth. To invest in the long-term usefulness of your ideas instead of the short-term dopamine of engagement. To evolve your voice instead of recycling your best-performing posts. It is slow. It is unglamorous. And it is the difference between work that flickers and work that forms a legacy.

And yes, the numbers might not reflect that right away. That's part of the dissonance of this season. You're doing some of your best work, but the charts don't move. You're more precise, more original, more confident, and yet less seen. But that is the nature of the plateau. It separates those who are building with vision from those who are building for validation. One is preparing for the next season. The other is trying to relive the last.

Eventually, though, something shifts. The silence gives way to insight. The internal pressure becomes clarity. The work begins to speak again, not louder, but deeper. It resonates in ways you couldn't have accessed without the stillness. And when the next wave of growth arrives, and it will, you'll be ready—not chasing and not scrambling. Just grounded. Clear. Present.

Because you didn't run from the plateau.

You built on it.

Chapter Fifteen: The Long Game

In an environment engineered for immediacy, long-term thinking is an act of resistance. Everywhere you turn, the system insists on urgency. Post now. React faster. Scale immediately. Optimize for today's trend. And if you're not growing at exponential rates, by the hour, by the post, you're told you're falling behind. This pressure doesn't just warp your behavior. It warps your expectations, your pacing, your sense of what meaningful progress looks like. It distorts the very way you think about success, luring you into a race that can't be won because it never ends. The algorithm has no finish line.

But there's a different path, if you're willing to walk it. A slower path. A quieter one. The path of the long game. It's not glamorous. It's not loud. It rarely wins the metrics war in the short term. But it is the only path that leads to sustainable creative independence. Because the long game is about building something that outlives the conditions it was born into, something that continues to matter, even as platforms change, audiences shift, and attention fragments.

To play the long game, you have to be willing to make tradeoffs. You have to sacrifice short-term popularity for long-term coherence. You have to choose depth over reach, clarity over speed, consistency over novelty. These choices rarely feel good in the moment. They can make you look out of step, even invisible. But they're what allow you to create work that lasts. Not because it went viral. But because it went deep.

Deep work doesn't care about the algorithm. It doesn't exist to game a system. It exists to serve an idea. To clarify a question. To

149

solve a real problem. It's not designed for maximum distribution. It's designed for maximum utility. And that utility is what gives it staying power. Because when something works, when it helps someone think more clearly, act more effectively, live more intentionally, they remember it. They come back to it. They share it. Not because you asked them to, but because the work earned it.

This is the paradox of the long game: the more you try to control your reach, the more fragile it becomes. But the more you focus on usefulness, the more your reach takes care of itself. Not instantly. Not predictably. But reliably, over time. Genuinely helpful ideas find their way into the right hands. They might not explode. But they persist. They travel not in waves of hype, but in chains of trust, passed from one person to another, not for entertainment, but for impact.

To create work that travels like that, you have to think beyond the content. You have to think about the context, the environment your reader is in, the decisions they're facing, and the blind spots they carry. You have to think about the systems your work is entering and ask: Will this survive outside my feed? Will this make sense six months from now? Will this still matter if I stop posting? These are uncomfortable questions for anyone addicted to immediacy. But they are essential if your goal is not just to be heard, but to be remembered.

And being remembered isn't about branding. It's not about having a catchy tagline or a signature aesthetic. It's about the repetition of meaning. When your ideas are grounded in something real, when they point to a consistent worldview, a set of values, a vision that doesn't shift with the tides, they start to accrue weight. People begin to associate your name not with a gimmick, but with a stance. With a way of thinking. With a level of rigor they can count on.

That kind of association doesn't happen overnight. It's built piece by piece, over years of showing up, refining, and returning. It's built not by launching louder, but by layering deeper. Each piece of work becomes part of a larger pattern. Each essay, each framework, each conversation reinforces the others. And slowly, your body of work becomes more than the sum of its parts. It becomes a terrain, something people can move through, return to, and orient themselves by.

To build that kind of terrain requires a shift in motivation. It's no longer about keeping up. It's about digging in. You stop measuring yourself against the pulse of the platform and start measuring yourself against the depth of your questions. You realize that the real competition isn't for visibility, it's for clarity. Clarity of purpose. Clarity of expression. Clarity of who you are and what you're trying to say. And that clarity only emerges when you stop chasing attention long enough to listen to your thinking.

Thinking, real thinking, takes time. It's not linear. It doesn't happen on a publishing schedule. Some of your best insights will arrive when you're not producing at all, when you're walking, reading, resting. That's another truth the culture doesn't like to admit: some of the most critical work happens offstage. It occurs in silence. It happens when you're not trying to be seen. And if you never allow for that silence, if you're constantly posting, always reacting, you rob yourself of the very clarity the long game requires.

So you learn to build margins into your practice. Space to observe. Space to doubt. Space to wander into territory that might not yield anything at first. These are not distractions. They are necessary detours. Because the long game is not a straight line, it is an unfolding, a gradual emergence of pattern and insight that cannot be forced. You can't schedule breakthroughs. But you can make room for them. And the more room you make, the more your work begins to reflect not just urgency, but wisdom.

Wisdom doesn't trend. It doesn't go viral. It doesn't fit neatly into reels or carousels. But it's what people come back to when the noise dies down, when the hype cycles fade. When they're tired of being optimized, entertained, and manipulated, they want something solid. Something human. Something that sees further than the next quarter. If your work can offer not just answers but perspective, you will never be irrelevant, even if you're quiet, even if you post less, even if your growth looks slow.

That slowness becomes a strength. Because while others burn out chasing the spike, you are building something that can last. You're not just capturing attention, you're compounding trust. And trust compounds more slowly than clicks, but it compounds far more powerfully. It's what makes people stick with you through the dips. It's what makes them seek you out even when you're not top of feed. And it's what turns a single post into a portal, an invitation into a deeper body of work.

Bodies of work are what the long game is really about. Not content calendars. Not social reach. Not engagement strategies. But the accumulation of thought. The stacking of insight. The construction of a coherent worldview that others can engage with, wrestle with, and build upon. This is not just content. This is intellectual infrastructure. And it's what allows your work to remain relevant even as the platforms that host it come and go.

That infrastructure, however, doesn't build itself. It takes care. It takes endurance. And it takes courage to resist constant reinvention. There's a temptation, especially when growth slows, to pivot into something flashier. To abandon the slow burn for a quick hit. But every time you do that, you fracture your foundation. You dilute your voice. You confuse your audience. The long game demands the opposite. It requires that you stay rooted even when the winds change. Not stagnant. Not rigid. But anchored.

Anchoring doesn't mean refusing to evolve. It means evolving from a clear center. A center that's been tested in quiet seasons. A center that's been defined not by trends, but by values. When your work is anchored in that kind of clarity, it can bend without a Master. It can grow without distorting. It can speak to new audiences without losing its original voice. That's how you become not just consistent, but resilient. And resilience, not virality, is what the long game rewards.

To play the long game well, you must come to terms with obscurity, not as a failure, but as a condition of freedom. Obscurity allows for experimentation. It grants you the latitude to explore without scrutiny, to make mistakes without magnification. And it is in those spaces, away from the feed, away from the audience, that you find your sharpest insights. The irony is that the work most capable of broad impact is often forged in the fire of private irrelevance. What feels like invisibility is, in hindsight, incubation.

This is why consistency is more important than momentum. Momentum fades. It's circumstantial. It's emotional. It depends on factors outside your control, what the market wants, what the algorithm favors, and what your audience happens to be craving this month. But consistency? That's internal. It's a habit. It's a posture. It's a form of trust, not in outcomes, but in process. When you keep showing up for work, even when no one's watching, you're building muscle. And when you do that over time, you're no longer at the mercy of external conditions. You're capable of enduring them.

That endurance is what separates the professionals from the performers. Performers ride the highs, then vanish in the lows. Professionals build even when the lights are off. They don't need to be inspired to execute. They don't need to be praised to persist. Their practice is a contract, with themselves, with their values, with the audience they haven't yet met. That kind of practice doesn't produce explosive results. It produces cumulative ones. Tiny insights stacked over time. Quiet decisions that add up to something unmistakably distinct.

And eventually, if you're lucky, or just stubborn enough to stick with it, that distinctiveness starts to speak for itself. You no longer have to chase the algorithm. The algorithm, slowly, begins to chase you. Not because you gamed it, but because you built something it couldn't ignore. Something too consistent, too practical, too real to overlook. You become a signal in a sea of noise. Not because you were louder, but because you were clearer. And clarity, once established, creates its gravity.

Gravity doesn't need to shout. It doesn't spike. It draws people in. It makes them stay. It makes them curious, not just about your content, but about your thinking. And that curiosity is what sustains attention over time. It's what turns readers into students. Students into clients. Clients into collaborators. It's not built on hacks or hooks. It's built on trust. Trust that you're going somewhere worth following. Trust that you won't disappear the moment the numbers dip.

That kind of trust is hard to earn, but once you have it, everything changes. You no longer have to explain your value. Your work does that for you. You no longer have to pitch every post. People arrive already primed, already receptive because the depth you've built over time has made you legible. Not trendy. Not novel. Legible. Your ideas are easy to follow, not because they're simplistic, but because they're structured. Your thinking is easy to reference, not because it's shallow, but because it's consistent.

Consistency, again, is the great differentiator. In a world chasing novelty, being consistent feels subversive. But it's what allows others to build on your work. To cite it, remix it, teach it. When your work becomes the raw material for other people's insights, you've moved beyond content. You've entered a contribution. And contribution, not visibility, is the true aim of the long game.

Because in the end, this isn't about building an audience. It's about creating a legacy. Not in the inflated, self-important sense, but in the quiet, durable way that matters. A legacy of clarity. A legacy of rigor. A legacy of showing up, not once, but over time. Not loudly, but precisely. Not perfectly, but persistently. A body of work that outlasts your moods. A presence that doesn't depend on performance. A voice that isn't just heard but remembered.

That is the long game. It is not for everyone. But it is for anyone willing to trade attention for impact. Anyone willing to build instead of brand. Anyone willing to be patient, precise, and profoundly helpful in a world obsessed with the opposite.

If you're still reading this, you are likely one of those people. And that means this isn't the end.

It's the beginning of a very different kind of relevance.

About the Author

Rowan Blake is a writer, strategist, and quiet rebel in the world of digital culture. With a background in media, design, and systems thinking, Rowan explores how modern creators can navigate visibility without losing their voice. Their work focuses on the intersection of technology and humanity, how algorithms shape behavior, how attention is captured and spent, and what it takes to stay grounded in a landscape that rarely stops moving.

Rowan writes for creators, entrepreneurs, and curious minds who care less about chasing trends and more about building something real. With a style that's reflective, sharp, and deeply personal, Rowan's books and essays help readers rethink the cost of constant optimization and imagine more sustainable, meaningful ways to create and connect.

Outside of writing, Rowan consults for values-driven startups, reads everything from neuroscience to speculative fiction, and occasionally disappears offline to recalibrate.

About the Publisher

Welcome to The Book On Publishing

At The Book On Publishing, we believe in rewriting the rules of learning. Whether you're chasing your next big idea, building a better life, or simply curious about what should have been taught in school, you've come to the right place.

We're a platform built for dreamers, doers, and lifelong learners, offering bold, practical books and tools that empower you to take charge of your journey. From real-world skills to mindset mastery, we publish the book on what matters.

No fluff. No lectures. Just what you need to know, delivered with clarity, purpose, and a spark of curiosity.

Start exploring. Start growing. Start writing your story.

Read more at https://thebookon.ca.

Acknowledgment of AI Assistance

Portions of this book were developed with the support of ChatGPT, an AI language model created by OpenAI. While every word has been carefully reviewed and refined by the author, ChatGPT served as a valuable tool for brainstorming, editing, and structuring ideas. Its assistance helped accelerate the creative process and bring clarity to complex topics.

www.ingramcontent.com/pod-product-compliance
Lightning Source LLC
Chambersburg PA
CBHW071649210326
41597CB00017B/2156